Mastery of the Mind

Mind

The Pathway to Empowerment

By: Jensen Monterrey, Inga Tara, Linda Campbell Gera, Amanda Scott, Beth An Schulz, Dr. Heather Ingbretson, Dean Afzal, Rahila Ali, Jerry Valerio, Dr. Laurie Emery, Tracy Carleton, Elizabeth Garvey, Joanne Klepal, Dr. Christine Anderson, Ronald Lance, Courtney Gale, Cynthia A. Isaac, Félicia "Faith" Hart, Michael Stevenson

Edited by: Elizabeth Garvey

Mastery of the Mind
The Pathway to Empowerment

Copyright © 2024 Authority Alliance Publishing
Published by Authority Alliance Publishing
www.AuthorityAlliance.co

ISBN-13: 978-1-946607-29-4
ISBN: 1-946607-29-0

10 9 8 7 6 5 4 3 2 1

Table of Contents

Introduction

Your mind is the most powerful supercomputer ever created, yet it comes without a user manual. Over the past fifty years, significant advances in "human technologies" have propelled us closer to mastering this incredible tool. Understanding how to operate your mind can transform your life in profound ways.

"Mastery of the Mind: The Pathway to Empowerment" is an essential guide crafted by nineteen leading experts across diverse fields—including Neuro-Linguistic Programming, psychology, hypnotherapy, success coaching, alternative health, and energy work. This collaboration brings together pioneering approaches and cutting-edge techniques that unlock the potential of the human mind.

This book is not just informational—it's a transformative tool that offers practical strategies and insights to help you harness your mental capabilities and reshape your life. Whether you seek personal growth, enhanced well-being, or greater professional achievement, "Mastery of the Mind" provides the knowledge and means to achieve your goals.

I hope this book leaves an indelible mark on your life that inspires others to master their minds, as well.

Michael Stevenson, May 2024
Authority Alliance Publishing

Mastery of the Mind

Achieve Your Goals with Focus and Discipline

By Jensen Monterrey, NLPMP, MTT, MHt, MSC, EFT

"...But do you know what it's like to give everything that you have? And push! And persevere!"–Marcus Elevation Taylor

Goals drive you to become better, to achieve the life you desire. Meaningful goals require that you push outside of your comfort zone, to take real action, to have focus and discipline. This drives your personal growth to reach your fullest potential and fulfill the life that you want.

Setting Compelling Goals

Goals need to be compelling, follow the S.M.A.R.T. principles, and be stated "as if now." In NLP, this makes goals effective and motivating.

S–simple, specific, see yourself, using sensory language

M–measurable, meaningful to you

A–as if now, achievable, all areas of your life

R–realistic, responsible / ecological

T–timed, toward what you want

Putting it all together would look like this:

It is now *(future date)*, and I *(am or have or do).*

I *(see, hear, and feel).*

As an example, I want to set a goal to lose 20 pounds in 10 weeks, so I want to go from 185 pounds to 165 pounds. This goal is specific, measurable (because I can weigh myself), achievable and realistic (because the National Institutes of Health recommend 1-2 pounds of weight loss per week to make it safe), and timed (10 weeks from now). If today is March 31, 2024, then 10 weeks from now would be June 9, 2024, and the goal would be written like this:

It is now *June 9, 2024*, and I *am 165 lbs*. I *see myself stepping on the scale and see that the scale reads 165 lbs., I hear myself saying, "Yes, I did it." I hear my family commending me and telling me how proud they are of me. I feel happy, energetic, motivated, and proud of myself.*

Future Pacing

To make the goal more compelling, it is important to visualize achieving the goal. Imagine looking at yourself in that future as if you were looking at yourself in a picture, seeing, hearing, and feeling achieving that goal. Make it as real as possible. This sets the unconscious mind on the path to make it possible.

Take Real Action

With the goal set, it is now time to take real action. Real physical action, for it is not enough to just think and dream about it. Real action means planning and executing the steps to achieve the goal.

I like to have a journal where I can write my goal, so that I can always see it. Then, I write my plan for the week, including the things that I must do for work, chores, and any other obligations. I will further break that down to what I need to do daily. That way, I can make sure that I can take care of my responsibilities so that I can then focus on the things I need to do to accomplish my goal. Without this, it's easy to get overwhelmed. Chunking it down makes the process more manageable.

I also recommend keeping a gratitude journal. To change yourself, you need to be grateful for who you are, what you have, and your accomplishments. You must first love yourself so that you can continue to grow and to let go of past regrets, negative emotions, and limiting beliefs.

Life is unpredictable and obstacles can get in your way, and so you must be able to adapt and adjust. What's important is to approach everything you do with a mindset of excellence.

There is no failure, only feedback. When something doesn't go as planned, or if you fall short, that means that you learn. Problems are challenges, and challenges provide you with opportunities to grow. As Thomas Edison said, "I have not failed. I've just found 10,000 ways that won't work." He could invent the light bulb because he did not give up and instead learned from what didn't work.

Cause vs. Effect

You can either live at cause or live at effect. Living at effect means letting external factors determine how you live your life, and blaming the things that are out of your control for your present state. Everything external to you is indeed out of your control. You can only control your own thoughts, emotions, and actions. Living at cause means you choose how you think, the decisions you make, and the actions you take.

To be successful, you must be at cause. You can cause your own results because you are empowered to control your mind and take action to achieve what you want.

Hakalau

Also known as "the learning state," "being in the zone," Hakalau is a technique used in NLP to enter a relaxed, receptive, focused state.

Achieving Hakalau is simple and easy:

1. Start by sitting on a comfortable chair, with your head pointing straight ahead.
2. Without moving your head, raise your eyes up about 20 degrees, as if to look at the space between your eyebrows, without strain, and focus on a spot on the ceiling or wall.
3. While focusing on the spot for at least 30 seconds but not more than 2 minutes, slowly allow your visual field to spread out as much as possible.

4. Now lower your eyes, while maintaining peripheral vision (expanded visual field).

You can enter Hakalau any time that you need to focus on the task at hand, while being in a relaxed, centered state.

Remember, though, tasks that require high focus and detail are best done with Foveal or Tunnel Vision. Hakalau can be used for most everything else.

Relaxation of the Mind and Body

Entering a relaxed state allows you to take control of your mind and to re-energize your body. With calm, focus, and energy, you can take on the challenges of the day, regardless of the situation. And just like physical training, mental training takes practice and time to master, and with discipline and dedication, it will yield amazing results.

Also, visualization or future pacing imagery, and auto suggestions (self-hypnosis), work better after entering a very relaxed state. That is the difference between positive self-talk (or affirmations) and self-hypnosis. Self-talk is done in the waking, alert state, and comprises short and repeated phrases. It is beneficial, but self-hypnosis is more powerful because it involves the subconscious mind. To perform self-hypnosis, you provide yourself with positive suggestions after entering the relaxed state.

My favorite way to relax is with Autogenic Training. I use it for visualization and self-hypnosis, to get a boost of calm and energy during the day, and to calm myself at night to get a deep and restful sleep.

Autogenic Training

1. In a sitting or lying position, with arms at the sides in a comfortable position, start by taking 10 slow even breaths using diaphragmatic breathing, while saying to yourself, "I am completely calm." At the end of each of the following steps, again say, "I am completely calm."
2. Focus your attention on your face. Repeat the following six or seven times: "The muscles of my face are completely smooth and relaxed."
3. Focus on your arms. Repeat the following six or seven times: "My arms are completely numb and heavy."
4. Keep your focus on your arms. Repeat the following six or seven times: "My arms are completely warm."
5. Focus on your legs. Repeat the following six or seven times: "My legs are completely numb and heavy."
6. Keep your focus on your legs. Repeat the following six or seven times: "My legs are completely warm."
7. Focus on your stomach. Repeat the following six or seven times: "My stomach is completely soft and warm."
8. Focus on your chest. Repeat the following six to seven times: "My heartbeat is calm and steady." Do this while also focusing on getting a feeling of warmth on your chest.
9. Focus on your forehead. Repeat the following six to seven times: "My forehead is pleasantly cool."

10. Now say to yourself, "I am completely calm and relaxed."

You can enjoy the feeling of relaxation, warmth, and heaviness, or perform visualization, or give yourself positive suggestions.

When you are finished, bring yourself to full alertness by saying (and doing): "Big stretch, deep breath, eyes wide open, feeling good and alert."

Fuel the Body and Brain

To reach your fullest potential, it's also important to keep your body and brain working at optimum levels. This means eating healthy, well-balanced meals and drinking lots of water.

Per the National Institutes of Health (NIH), healthy, well-balanced meals should comprise the three macronutrients with a distribution range of 35-45% carbohydrate, 10-35% protein, and 20-35% fat. The optimum proportion will depend on your activity levels and physique goals. Carbohydrates should comprise fruits, vegetables, dairy, or whole grains. Proteins from lean meats, fish, and poultry. Good unsaturated fats from nuts, seeds, fish, and vegetable oils. Consult a nutritionist for guidance.

The NIH also recommends a daily fluid intake of 8 cups per day for women and 10 cups per day for men. Water should make up most of the fluid intake to support body functions.

Putting it All Together

One way to put all this together daily would look like this:

1. Upon waking up and after taking care of any biological needs, drink a full cup of water.
2. Go into Hakalau and write a few things you are thankful for in your gratitude journal.
3. While in Hakalau review or write your plan for the day.
4. Do Autogenic Training and once relaxed visualize (future pace) having achieved your goals for the day and be proud of it. Give yourself positive suggestions.
5. Eat a healthy breakfast, lunch, and dinner, with plenty of water.
6. As you complete the tasks for the day, cross them out or put a check mark next to them. Use Hakalau, as necessary.
7. During breaks, take time to fully recharge by doing additional Autogenic Training. This can include positive auto suggestions and visualization.
8. I also like to do Autogenic Training and visualization just before working out, to get a boost of energy and motivation.
9. At the end of the day, look at your daily plan and feel proud to have completed your tasks for the day. If you could not do all of it, don't beat yourself up about it, instead learn from it, then adapt and adjust accordingly.
10. Prioritize sleep. A good restful sleep allows your body and brain to recover, so you can be ready for the next

day. If you have difficulty falling asleep, then do Autogenic Training.

Of course, there are other ways to achieve relaxation, and learning about alternate methods gives you more choices.

With focus and discipline, you can easily and effortlessly make this a part of your daily routine. Focus on excellence, be at cause, and realize your fullest potential.

About Jensen Monterrey, NLPMP, MTT, MHt, MSC, EFT

Jensen Monterrey is a distinguished professional with dual bachelor's degrees in industrial and electronics engineering. His thirst for knowledge and excellence propelled him further, leading to achieving dual master's degrees in engineering management and electrical engineering.

Jensen's professional journey is marked by significant achievements and his approach combines a deep technical understanding with a visionary perspective, always aiming to push the boundaries of what's possible.

Jensen's passions extend beyond the confines of engineering. His endeavors as a former competitor in athletics and a current powerlifting athlete have instilled in him the importance of mental and physical harmony, leading him to explore the realms of mental training.

Intrigued by the profound impact of mindset on performance, Jensen delved into Neuro-Linguistic Programming (NLP), becoming a Master Practitioner. This journey into NLP was not just a pursuit of personal mastery, but a pathway to empower others. Blending his engineering mindset with insights into the human mind, Jensen is driven by a compelling vision to help individuals unlock their full potential.

Get Jensen's free gift: www.mind-book.net/gift/Jensen

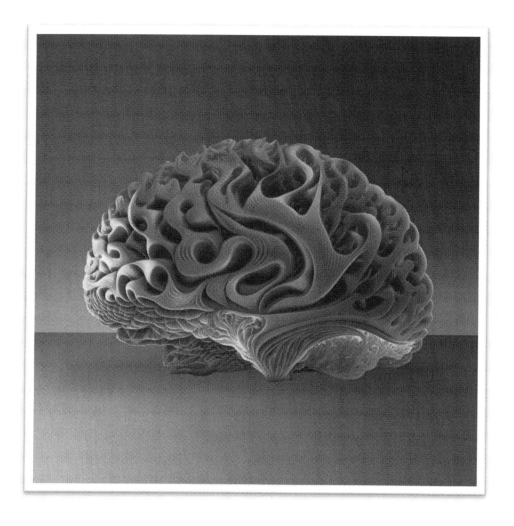

Mastery of the Mind

The Mindset Reset
The Power of Mental Detox to Achieve Balance and Happiness
By Inga Tara, MS, CCHt, LC

The mind-body-spirit connection is essential to achieving balance and healing in life, whether facing health challenges, relationship struggles, stress, burnout, or low self-worth.

Addressing all aspects, including physical, mental, emotional, and spiritual dimensions, is a key to vitality and happiness. It's the *foundation* you need to learn for your well-being, just like learning to walk before engaging in sports.

While a healthy diet and staying active promote a longer and healthier life, remember you are more than a mere physical being. Every aspect of your being, including your consciousness, thoughts, and emotions, is *your responsibility* and affects you profoundly. So nurturing *positive thoughts and mental habits* is paramount in shaping your life.

It's important to harness the power of the subconscious mind in this journey.

Your subconscious stores every experience, influencing your deepest perceptions and behaviors, and your positive thoughts have the transformative potential to change the course of your life.

So, creating a practice of *mental detox* is crucial.

19

Your Internal Dialog: Negative and Positive Self-Talk

The Book of Proverbs says, "As the men think, so is he." It's not what happens to you, but how you react to your thoughts and emotions. The mind's power plays an enormous role in overall happiness, requiring you to focus on positivity to stay on track to achieve balance and happiness.

Think of it as turning on the TV to watch the "Happiness" channel. Deviating even slightly changes the effect–channels before or after could be news, violence, or politics. Tuning your mind to "happiness" leads your body to follow suit.

You have the ability and free will to decide and choose. Keep your mind tuned for happiness by keeping it healthy with good choices and decisions. By choosing not to change, you end up tuning to a different TV channel.

How do you balance your mind? Start with an internal dialog of *critical thinking*.

Your inner voice or critic is a community of voices talking to you, negating, refuting, putting you down, and criticizing you. Most of that internal dialog is negative, *making you your worst critic.* How many times have you looked in the mirror and criticized yourself for being fat, unattractive, wearing the wrong clothes, or having bad hair? To achieve positive mental well-being, you must fight these voices with positive self-talk.

What you say to yourself matters. As a perfectionist, I know firsthand how it feels to judge yourself. So, when your inner critics show up, thank them for their efforts to protect you and move to another thought.

Tools for Dealing with Negative Self-Talk

Research shows you have 6,200 thoughts a day. Most of them are repetitive, and 80% are negative. You have 6.5 thoughts per minute, and each thought gives you the choice between being positive or negative.

This gives you tremendous power. What happens when you constantly think negatively or tell yourself the same negative story? "My parents never loved me; they treated my sibling better than me," or "I'm not lucky in a relationship. My boyfriend cheated on me and will do it again. I can't trust him." These thoughts keep you stuck in this story, reliving it. And your subconscious believes it's the only way your life can unfold.

Cancel-Cancel is the negative thought-stopping technique I recommend to my clients. It's like what Scarlet O'Hara from Gone with the Wind says: "I will think about it tomorrow."

It's normal for worries and negative thoughts to arise. But when you realize them, interrupt the pattern by saying, "Cancel, cancel!" Replace it with a positive thought or release it to think about later, allowing space for an alternative positive thought.

You cannot stop negative thoughts from occurring, but you can have a replacement phrase ready. Say, "I am happier, healthier, and more relaxed than ever before," "The Universe knows what I need and will take good care of me," or any affirmation *believable to you*, repeating it 25-30 times a day.

Reframe Your Thoughts. Is it a glass half full or half empty? Whose choice is it? It's yours! You *get to decide for yourself* whether to call something a *problem or an opportunity*. Eliminate negative language and thoughts by shifting to a positive perspective - a perspective of learning new skills of positive thinking, reprogramming your mind, and embracing deeper spiritual lessons that foster soul growth. Whatever it is, reframe your thoughts and substitute them with more positive ones.

Be the Guardian of Your Mind. Evaluate everything you put into your mind and keep the junk out. You may encounter negative influences, like a co-worker or relative bringing you down. But you can choose not to subject yourself to negativity *willingly*.

How you see the world is shaped by your thoughts and influenced by factors like television, social media, and your acquaintances. It's important to be very strict about what energy you allow into your life.

Just like a bouncer controls entry to a club, you decide who gets in and who doesn't. Evaluate what you consume - all forms of media, interactions, and entertainment impact your thoughts and feelings. Your time is precious, so why waste it on junk that doesn't move you toward your goals?

Your attention directs your life force. Notice how you feel after watching a feel-good movie versus a violent one - they affect your subconscious with vastly different vibrations and messages.

I bet you can recall scary scenes and soundtracks from old movies like "Jaws" or "Psycho" as they are embedded in your mind, but you won't remember a compliment from last month. Why is that? Your brain has a primitive part designed to protect you from real or imaginary threats. Those big-screen traumatic events trigger your subconscious to believe what you tell it at that moment, not able to differentiate between real or not, archiving and cataloging them for your protection. On the other hand, positive compliments are not seen as life-threatening, so they are forgotten faster.

Create your own criteria for what you allow into your mind. I avoid watching the news to avoid its negativity and choose movies that are uplifting, educational, growth-oriented, inspiring, or contribute to my self-improvement journey.

Traumatic events you see get locked in your brain forever, so strive for a positive mental environment.

Learn a Mind-Calming Technique. Learn to switch off your mind, relax, and live a life in a more serene place.

> Take a deep breath, close your eyes, and imagine stepping into your mind, noticing how it feels and looks. What do you see?

Imagine a special switch that instantly relaxes your muscles when it's off, allowing you to unwind effortlessly. Find that switch and turn it off, knowing you're in control and can switch it back on whenever needed. Feel the deep relaxation and calmness.

There's another switch in this mind space that quiets racing thoughts. Find it and turn it off to enjoy this deep relaxation, peace, and calm.

When you're ready, turn the switches back on.

With some practice, you can get instant results, which will help you maintain a positive mental attitude.

Happiness isn't what happens to you, but your reaction to thoughts and emotions. Since your thoughts shape your life and reality, it's important to detach from them, gaining a greater level of awareness before reacting and preventing unnecessary fights, trauma, and misery.

While you can't change the people or situations that come your way, you can choose your responses. It's a simple matter of choosing between **stimulus and response**. The stimulus is never the problem; it's your mind that determines your response - positively or negatively.

Every thought gives you a choice of what you say to yourself, so fill your mind with the good stuff that truly matters.

When deciding what to put into your mind, consider these questions. Is it positive and uplift you or bring you down? Will it make you a better person or diminish you? Can it help you grow or hinder you? Will it align you with your desired life or not? Take time each day to fill your mind with positivity, happiness, joy, health, and abundance.

Focus on What You Want. In a state of gratitude, act like you already have it. Most people think about what they don't want in life, but you might settle for anything this way. Instead, create a mental picture of what you *want* from your life and your relationship. Write all your fears, find alternatives to them, and focus on how you want to feel instead - this is a self-act.

Create a clear picture of your ideal life in detail, including how you want to feel overall and in your body: health, wealth, relationships, mental, emotional, social, and spiritual. Otherwise, life and relationships will just *happen to you* instead of *you creating* what you want in your life.

Use Affirmations. The simple self-hypnosis technique you can do is affirming positive statements about you and your life to retrain your mind. This powerful method, found in many good books on the power of the subconscious mind, shows how affirmations change negative, self-defeating thoughts.

Record affirmations on your phone and listen 2-3 times daily while in a light trance state, preferably first thing in the morning or just before falling asleep.

Start a Journal. Journaling is a tool for enhancing self-awareness and mental clarity, gaining insights, heightening self-esteem, and improving sleep. Journaling and meditation can help *resolve painful relationship issues*.

Think of one thing or person who "pushes your buttons" and write it down. On the spiritual level, these people are often a challenge your soul has in this incarnation to learn the lesson of open-mindedness and forgiveness.

Ask for Divine support and guidance. Then, move into a relaxing state before writing about the issue from three perspectives: your own, the other person's perspective, and from a *neutral* observer's view, the Divine Witness. Looking at the situation this way helps you see how it changes your response.

Create a Gratitude Diary. Regularly practicing gratitude is a fantastic practice that fosters happiness and inner peace and helps you appreciate life's little joys and successes. Embracing gratitude makes it easier to enjoy the positive emotions that bring a greater source of happiness.

Including "states" called joy, love, and gratitude in your daily life makes it virtually impossible to feel negative emotions. A state of gratitude floods your brain with serotonin, so it's difficult to be depressed and grateful simultaneously. I encourage clients to write 5 to 10 things they are grateful for every day.

Use Meditation. It is one of my favorite tools for mental detox. Over 18,000 studies show that meditation has many benefits, including relieving emotional and mental toxicity, reducing stress, and reducing negative thoughts and feelings. Consistent 20-30-minute meditation helps concentrate and focus the mind and activate areas in the brain associated with happiness and compassion.

Meditation types range from breathing and mindfulness to mantra, walking, or visualization; just choose what resonates with you best and be consistent. My personal favorite is guided imagery, which creates complete relaxation of the body and mind while images and feelings arise and positively influence the subconscious mind.

How you react to situations and the stories you tell yourself determines your happiness. Mastering meditative techniques will allow you to transcend problems and find joy in being still, silent, and breathing. Download my meditation in this chapter and try it.

Your mind gravitates to familiar ways of thinking and feeling. Breaking free from decades of negative self-talk requires effort, focus, and motivation. *Practice* having positive thoughts about the people you love and all aspects of your life for a balanced lifestyle full of happiness, love, and fulfillment.

The world is a complicated place, and it is rare to live a well-lived life without regrets and traumas. The good news is that *you have the power* to shape your thoughts, create a more positive mindset, and transform your life for the better.

About Inga Tara, MS, CCHt, LC

 Inga is a Love and Relationship Coach, Healer, and Clinical Hypnotherapist at IngaTara.com. She is passionate about helping women transform their mindsets and embrace self-worth. Through her business, Self-Mastery Vortex, Inga helps clients overcome the barriers that hinder their ability to become their best versions and establish loving relationships with their partners, themselves, and others.

Inga has a Master of Science degree and graduated from Southwest Institute of Healing Arts with a Diploma in Mind-Body Wellness and Board Certifications in Life Coaching, Clinical Hypnotherapy, Holistic Nutrition, and Reiki Master.

Focusing on achieving balance and harmony among the mind, body, and spirit, Inga specializes in honing relationship skills, self-mastery, leadership skills, and practicing meditation and energy work.

Inga's personal experience and expertise in various holistic modalities allow her to help women conquer their fears, challenges, and insecurities and make positive life changes.

With a warm and compassionate approach, her goal is to inspire and assist women to create their best lives by exploring personal development and spirituality in a simple and accessible way.

Get Inga's free gift: www.mind-book.net/gift/Inga

Mastery of the Mind

NLP Role Models for Effective Parenting

By Linda Campbell Gera, NLPMP, MTT, MHt, MSC, EFT

Many years ago, when I first became a parent, I realized there was no parent training class, zero training other than "hands on" and role modeling from our parents. My mom learned her parenting behavior and skills from her parents. Her mother was fifteen when she was born and, from my experience, 15-year-olds are still children themselves. My mom role modeled her parents who had learned no true parenting skills.

How we parent is a learned behavior. We take on the parenting skills of our parents, right, wrong, positive, or negative. Since my mother's mom resorted to yelling and used passive aggressive language and behavior, that is what my mom learned and then how she raised us. My mom was the disciplinarian since my dad, who was at work every day, only stepped in when things got out of hand. Neither had any idea that their parenting skills needed a serious upgrade.

I would have to say that the hardest behavior to recover from was passive aggressive language and how belittling it was. The nasty things my mom said out of anger were difficult to hear. As we grew up, some fights were terrible. As a child, I knew nothing about this behavior or how to address it. I want to point out that even with this behavior, when my mother was not on the "war path," as we called it, she was a very loving mother. My childhood was happy, and I felt loved. It was only when my mom lost her temper, things went sideways. I knew passive aggressive behavior was not something I wanted to use in my life, so it was easier for me to let go and not pass it onto my child. That type of behavior always left me feeling dirty, and I cringed when I heard other people using it. Once I overheard a friend talking this way to her fiancé. I was sad for both, as I knew their marriage would not last, and it did not.

The behavior that was harder to change and let go of was the yelling. Recognizing after raising my son that this style of parenting was not the best approach, I desired to do things differently as a grandparent, but I just was not sure how. Fortunately, later in life, I got the chance to change. My partner and I got into a minor disagreement. Faced with the choice to learn to stay calm, not yell or raise my voice when angry, or the relationship would be over, I changed.

Grateful for this life lesson to this day, it was important for me to learn. It served as a wake-up call, and I learned to stay calm. Despite not being perfect, and still getting triggered occasionally, I could let go of that old behavior pattern, and it only took 50 years. **Neuro-Linguistic Programming** (NLP) could have helped me to let go of this much quicker, but I had not found it yet.

I learned about NLP when I first attended a Tony Robbins event in 2016. By 2020, I signed up for a class. It was fun, but the class did not provide enough time to earn a certification and it was independent study. This material was too new and figuring it out on my own was not the best approach. So, although I got a "taste" of it, I had to keep looking for the right training.

In 2021, I took an online hypnotherapy class which was very well done, and I learned a lot. I had earned a hypnotherapy certification in the 90s, but this material and information was much more detailed and included the history which lends so much more credibility. In 2022, when they offered an in-person class, I signed up. It was in this class that I signed up to take both NLP certifications and become a certified NLP Trainer. This company knew how to conduct training. In just the first NLP class, I learned things I could use in my relationships and I started focusing on how I could use it at work and at home with my granddaughter.

My granddaughter, Aurora, was born in 2019, and she is my joy. I love spending time with her and if you remember having young children, they can be a joy and a handful.

I started using NLP with Aurora when she was about three. At first it was at bedtime, changing the tone of my voice, and talking to her in a soothing way to put her to sleep faster. As she got a little older, I would use **pattern interrupt** to change and redirect her focus.

This proved immensely helpful when she would throw a dreaded tantrum. She would focus on something she wants and throw a fit, then I interrupted her focus using tone of voice, humor, or something unexpected instead of yelling and making the tantrum worse. I was quite successful in getting her to redirect her focus. Sometimes it would take longer than others and I had to stay calm and patient, all the while she was yelling and crying. I noticed I was having success with her, and I encouraged my son to learn better parenting skills than what I taught him as a child. So, he also took an NLP class.

Making mistakes can be a great learning opportunity. Encouraging kids that making mistakes is normal and a chance to learn and grow boosts their self-esteem. Now when Aurora makes a mistake, she says "Nana, It's Okay" and I ask her, "What can we learn from this?" so she gets the full lesson.

Another technique is using **Positive Language**. Remember, "Don't spill the milk?" That statement is not used in our house because what happens when you say it? The milk gets spilled! Instead, we use, "Please hold on to your glass." Instead of, "Don't run," it is "Walk slowly." Changing the language you use enables children to focus on the desired behavior instead of trying to avoid negative behavior.

The words used are important. Changing how and when I use these two words, "can't" and "don't," can impact a child's behavior and future growth. Reframing can't statement from "I can't" to "I will do my best", or "I am still learning" empowers children and enables them to focus on their effort and progress rather than bringing attention and focus on their limitations.

Using the word "don't" can get people to focus on what they don't want instead of what they want. Try it. For example, if I say, "Don't focus on that bump on your arm," you will focus on your arm and try to find a bump! Never ask for what you don't want, only ask for what you want. This works with children as well as adults. Our subconscious mind only processes "spill the milk." It does not process negatives like the word "don't." When you change your language, you change the behavioral response to it.

I love encouraging **problem solving**, and Aurora is already interested in helping. When we discuss how to solve a simple problem, such as where to put something away in the house or where to put her toys, she wants to help solve it. She starts with "Nana, I have an idea." It is so pure and thoughtful. I nurture this and ask her to tell me her idea. It may be nothing we can use, but just listening and encouraging her lets her know we value her. Sometimes she comes up with great ideas! Practicing problem solving with children encourages critical thinking, which is something we can certainly use more of these days.

Another useful technique is **giving children choices**. It sounds so simple, and I did not learn this from my parents. Yet it is so important! Aurora is turning five, and she wants to show everyone that she can do things herself. When we prepare food for lunch or dinner, she can be picky, so I give her choices; "Do you want broccoli or asparagus?" "Chicken with ketchup or chicken with ranch?" It empowers her and gives her the feeling she has some control.

Toddlers and beyond need to explore and try things on their own. Aurora, for example, does not want help when she is trying to figure out something new. We need to give them time to think through the process, to focus on the task instead of jumping in to help. As parents and grandparents, we are always in a hurry to get where we need to go or to finish something before starting something new. We may rush or dismiss a child when they are trying to learn something for themselves, and we need to give them space and allow them to do it. I have observed Aurora when an adult steps in to do it for her and she becomes upset, which I totally understand. We took away an important learning opportunity!

A good example is when Aurora wanted to unlock the belt of her car seat and get out of it on her own. She knew how to do it; it took practice with the amount of pressure on the release button, and she just needed patience and encouragement to make it happen. Now, I encourage her and say, "Why don't you try to figure it out?" and she gets excited. It is like I have given her an opportunity to learn something new. Next time you want to figure something out or learn something new, just focus and practice and don't let anyone do it for you!

Toddlers are just learning how to control and handle their emotions and they can get very overwhelmed. It all starts when you introduce the word "no." Their emotions overwhelm them, and they have a tantrum. Acknowledging a child's emotions, especially when she has been told no, can be a challenge. I have learned to **acknowledge her emotions** by using statements like; "I understand you are feeling frustrated (or angry) right now." Acknowledging these emotions and not dismissing them can help children let go and move forward.

Another tool I will share is **building rapport**. One technique I use with Aurora, for building rapport, is called **Mirroring and Matching**. Mirroring and matching your body language, your tone of voice, or your facial expressions to your child can quickly bring you into rapport. When you are in rapport, they will listen to you more actively. I have watched Aurora do this naturally when she plays with other children, and I will continue guiding her in this direction.

This last example was the most important opportunity to use NLP with my granddaughter. Aurora had trouble with specific sounds when she was learning to talk. A speech therapist determined she had a sub-mucosal cleft palate. That is a hole that never closed in your soft palate or the roof of your mouth. Without surgery, should not speak clearly.

When she was four, she had surgery. I was genuinely concerned about the fear that can be associated with going into the hospital, being probed and prodded, and being in pain after surgery.

This fear came from my childhood when I was in and out of the hospital with asthma and nearly died. I remember a time when I woke up all alone in the hospital room at age seven. We had come in through the ER in the middle of the night, and my parents had to leave to take one parent back home to be with my three siblings. This was back in the 60s when they had oxygen tents for asthmatics, which was a big plastic square box over your head and torso. It had zippers on the sides to use for hospital care and to talk to the patient.

Leaving me with an IV in my arm and very weak, nobody thought to leave the nurse's button within reach. Waking up, I found myself all alone in the room, with dimmed lights in the hallway. Feebly calling out to my parents, and then for anyone to answer me, nobody heard. I quickly tired, and fell back asleep. Upon waking again, one of my parents was back in the room. Never forgetting that experience, I held onto that abandonment issue, which affected my adult relationships until I discovered NLP. NLP helped me to let go of the abandonment, for which I am incredibly grateful.

I wanted to make sure my granddaughter's experienced was nothing like mine and that she would come through her surgery unscathed, happy, and smiling. I debated on how to handle this type of experience as she was so young. After discussing it with fellow NLP Practitioners, I used hypnosis as a metaphorical story. A psychiatrist, Milton Erickson, pioneered **metaphorical hypnosis**. He was a successful hypnotherapist and a genius in this style. Most of his clients would come to his office and he would tell them a story and send them on their way. They were unaware that the story he told them would subconsciously address their issue.

Metaphorical stories can speak directly to the unconscious to facilitate transformative change. I learned it in my NLP Hypnosis class. Aurora loves storytelling, so the day before the surgery I told her a metaphorical story intended to help make her feel safe and loved during the entire hospital and surgical process.

Her hospital stay went smoothly, and the hypnotic story worked very well. Aurora never appeared or even mentioned she was scared. She took the surgery in stride and appears to have had no residual side effects. She had little pain and healed quickly and has been talking up a storm ever since! Two weeks later, we had to go back to the doctor for a follow up. There was no hesitation in her. She hopped on the table and let the doctor look in her mouth. That visit came and went as if she had never had surgery!

In comparison, when I had to see the doctor when I was sick or after hospital visits, I never wanted to go and threw a fit for my parents. I associated the doctor with the abandonment, and of course, needles. Fortunately, Aurora does not!

There's a lot more I could share, so I hope this has inspired you to check out NLP. To encourage you to take a class and learn these powerful techniques, I am going to offer you a free recording of my EFT mini class. I hope to see you in one of my classes soon!

About Linda Campbell Gera, NLPMP, MTT, MHt, MSC, EFT

 Linda Lee Campbell Gera is a seasoned Master Hypnotherapist, NLP practitioner, Trainer and Success Coach with over seven years of dedicated coaching experience.

Armed with certifications in Coaching, Hypnotherapy, and NLP from esteemed institutions like Transform Destiny, Linda is a beacon of transformative personal growth.

Specializing in guiding successful career women through significant life changes, Linda empowers her clients to shed old narratives and negative emotions, paving the way for more fulfilling and prosperous lives. She customizes her approach, guiding each individual on a path of self-discovery and empowerment.

Driven by a fervent desire to see others thrive, Linda is renowned for her compassionate and effective coaching style. With a track record of countless success stories and gratified clients, Linda's dedication to personal growth and transformation speaks volumes.

At New Me Transformation, Linda's warm, empathetic nature and ability to put people at ease, combined with her expertise, positions her as a trusted ally in the quest for self-improvement.

Get Linda's free gift: www.mind-book.net/gift/Linda

Mastery of the Mind

Master Your Mind

Overcoming Self-Sabotage

By Amanda Scott, MA, LCPC, NCC

What would you say to feel certain and confident that your responses to life would be effective and successful? How is it possible, you may ask? You can and will experience a difference when you make the choice to practice mastering your mind.

To master the mind, it is essential to have an accurate awareness of how you are functioning. You must step out of pride or ego, and you may have to step out of your comfort zone to gain a realistic perspective on how your strategies are working.

A year ago, this would have meant something quite different to me, and I would have logically and methodically laid out the common self-sabotage tendencies and how to overcome them. However, in this last year, I was blinded by my self-sabotage and gained important insight into how deceiving and un-serving self-sabotage can be.

Last year started with my mother becoming terribly ill in response to her chemotherapy. If you have served in a care-giver role, you know the conflicting roller coaster that accompanies. You feel exhausted, powerless, and overwhelmed; you yo-yo, from I cannot do another thing to I am not doing enough.

It got so bad that we interviewed for hospice care. However, my mother became so disenchanted with the choices, she decided it would be easier to live. Amazingly, she regained her strength and, by the beginning of summer, was living independently and nearly back to her usual self. I wish the story would stop there and I would describe what I learned from that.

However, I took the opportunity of her regaining her independence to check on myself. It had been a stressful six months and wanted to ensure it had not impacted my health. I was expecting to find I was anemic—and I was. What I was not expecting was my cancer diagnosis, but I had that news too. Thus began my imposter syndrome and self-sabotage.

I was conflicted. It was still so fresh in my mind how sick my mother was, how everyone looked at her with that sympathetic face, and spoke with a tone of despair. I did not want that. So, no one was going to know about this since I was not "sick" enough for any of that, anyway. I did not think I deserved that kind of attention. I followed all the medical recommendations and instructions: countless mammograms, four biopsies, two lumpectomies, weeks of radiation, and starting what will be years on a medication. Even here I breeze over the process. Only three people knew, and I missed only two days of work. My attitude stayed positive, my energy stayed up, and I met all my responsibilities. That was until I hit the space where I could not take on another thing. I was empty and depleted. Can you see my self-sabotage?

I was overcompensating; ignoring my physical and emotional needs for rest and support and it negatively affected my treatment. Every step of the way needed extra steps until I accepted that I needed support and encouragement to get through this journey.

The Forms of Self-Sabotage

To keep things simple, overcompensation is one of three ways you can ineffectively respond to a stressful situation. There are even two ways to overcompensate.

For myself, I denied my needs that would interrupt my routine and dove into a positive work attitude. This fits the perfectionist, superhero, and/or soloist type. The "I can keep doing better and I do not need help" mindset.

You could go the other direction and purposely make a mess of things. The metaphorical setting fire, for if you set the fire, then you cannot fail or be disappointed—you chose this outcome.

Both offer a feeling of control and stem from perfectionistic tendencies and fear of failure—and possibly fear of success.

Another self-sabotage form is surrender. With this, you passively accept whatever negative belief you may hold about your situation and act accordingly. Making you in effect of your environment and taking no responsibility or accountability for yourself. You give up your control and lean into believing the negative belief. Again, there is a fear of failure. Not working against the negative belief provides a near sense of comfort. There also is a lack of self-awareness, specifically in how surrender is a sabotage that discounts your strengths.

The third form is avoidance, as it would suggest, you would avoid any situation that may trigger a stress response. This is a coping mechanism. Fueled by procrastination, this protective strategy prevents you from ever having to fail, for you never get into any action.

All three responses suggest there is a flow of negative self-talk that is questioning or outright denying your abilities, strengths, and values. Arguably, worse than self-doubt, this mindset limits your belief system. You feel you are not good enough to deserve success. It is an inaccurate feeling, and that part does not matter in the moment the feeling is experienced.

Where does Self-Sabotage Originate?

So, what leads to these self-sabotage behaviors? It may have been your family environment. Who were your household role models? What messages did you receive from them? Was there too much encouragement or praise? Or was the opposite true and there was harsh critical or punitive feedback? Your family environment can give a strong modeling system for how to manage stressors.

Social pressure can also be a factor. What messages do you believe society is sending to you about who you need to be? Who is deciding how you should live your life? Is what you are doing important to you? I won't go down the social media rabbit-hole, but what are you exposing yourself to? Is it helping your motivation towards goals or making you feel unworthy?

Your sense of belonging or lack there of can impact how you respond to stress. Are you trying to fit in and feeling like a puzzle piece is not going into place? Do you have that group of others that get you? You are a mammal and need your pack for your well-being.

Your innate personality type may predispose you to choose one of these responses in your default setting. Those identified as Type A are more likely than our Type B friends to have more perfectionistic thinking and fear failure. Or in Myers Briggs terms, the judgers are more prone than the perceivers. Though self-sabotage is fair game for all.

I want to validate your experience—and my own. Now that you can connect with your self-sabotage experience, focus on how to overcome it, and master your mind.

Overcoming Self-Sabotage

There are many strategies to help combat self-sabotage. You can start by seeking trusted feedback. Who in your life can provide you with genuine, non-punitive evidence to help you grow your own self-awareness? Is there someone who provides you with helpful insight? Keep an open, curious mind and hear how others experience you—use the feedback to make the changes you want.

Practicing mindfulness is highly effective. The practice of mindfulness is attending to the present moment—connecting with what stimuli your senses are experiencing without judgment. This practice can calm the stress response and break the pattern of negative thinking. Mindfulness practice also allows you to master what you are attending to, giving you control of what captures your focus.

A game changer for perfectionistic tendencies and fear of failure is shifting your perspective regarding failure. When failure is reframed to feedback or learning what is needed to be successful, it feels quite different. Failure feels like a closed door, a dead end. Feedback is more like a detour. You will no longer take the route you were first planning, and you will still arrive at your destination. I know you can see how powerful this can be for your motivation.

You also need to get out of rumination—the stewing in negative emotions. This mental action is un-serving and unhelpful, reliving the negative state without effective processing. Remember, there is no failure, there is feedback. So, there should be no rumination, only reflection. With reflection, you mindfully review what worked. What should be repeated? What needs to be changed? How do you want to change it? What are the facts? What messages are your emotions giving you? Reflection will serve you well.

It is important to practice being kind to yourself, to have self-compassion. This is not letting go of accountability or letting yourself off the hook. This is treating yourself like you would your dearest best friend. Listen to what you are saying to yourself and if you would not speak that way to a friend, don't speak that way to yourself!

A sneaky way you fall prey to self-sabotage is when you lose focus on your values. Are you in need of reconnecting to your values? Your values are dynamic and change throughout your life. Perhaps you are focusing on a value that is no longer of interest. You may benefit from a value reappraisal. When your actions are congruent with your true values, you feel good about your efforts.

When you understand the voice and how it works to protect you, you can hear it differently. All the self-sabotage messages stem from a positive intention to preserve the self. In your life, it served you very well and now it is time to see how you can change it to better serve your needs. You have the brain to recognize that now is not then, and it is time for a new message and new actions.

Put It All Together

In conclusion, you want to practice self-compassion and know how to self-soothe. That is showing yourself the kindness you would your best friend and selecting actions that go against your maladaptive coping habits. Maladaptive habits feel great in the moment and then have you feeling worse in the more long-term. You will know if you are following an un-serving pattern if you feel guilt, shame, or overall disappointment with your actions.

Be honest with yourself about both your strengths and limitations. Perfection is fraudulent. It both limits your potential and does not exist for humans. When you are so focused on getting it right, you often miss the brilliant ideas that come with an amount of risk. When you focus on the outcomes of your actions, you receive guidance on how to reach your goals. You evolve from your mistakes, continuing to develop to a more ideal self.

You must ditch negative self-talk. This includes those doubting thoughts that stop you before you start and that pesky rumination that has you feel negative emotions with no guidance on how to improve the situation. The goal is not to control what thoughts pop up, but to control which thoughts you attend to. With practice, the thoughts you attend to will be the thoughts that continue to generate, so make sure they are helpful. Remember, your language does not describe your experience, it determines it.

With these practices, I know you will recognize the improvements in minimizing self-sabotage and reaching your full potential.

At the time of this writing, I am cancer free—though still anemic. I continue working on being honest about my strengths and limitations. Specifically, focusing on what I need to function at my best level. Taking time each week to reflect on how I am using and replenishing my energies.

You, too, will benefit from creating this new relationship with yourself. Take time to listen to your authentic needs and ignore the anxious or critical charges against yourself. Allow yourself to make effective choices for your success. You know what you need most and when you listen, you will respond accordingly.

About Amanda Scott, MA, LCPC, NCC

 Amanda Scott, a licensed Clinical Professional Counselor and Success Coach with 15 years of experience, is dedicated to helping individuals navigate life's transitions and reach their full potential.

Amanda's accomplishments include being a National Certified Counselor, Certified ADHD professional (ADHD-CCSP), Certified Clinical Anxiety Treatment Professional (CCATP), Master Practitioner of NLP, Learning Behavioral Specialist, and a best-selling author. Her extensive training and certifications allow her to provide comprehensive support to those facing challenges such as ADHD, anxiety, and other mental health concerns.

Through her business, Manda's PathWay, and a clinician at Dayrise Wellness, Amanda offers a unique and personalized approach to counseling and coaching. She is passionate about helping individuals discover their life's purpose, overcome obstacles, set goals, and achieve success in all areas of their lives. With Amanda's guidance and commitment, her clients' well-being and growth shines through in her work, making her a trusted and valuable resource for those seeking support on their journey to personal development and achievement.

Get Amanda's free gift: www.mind-book.net/gift/Amanda

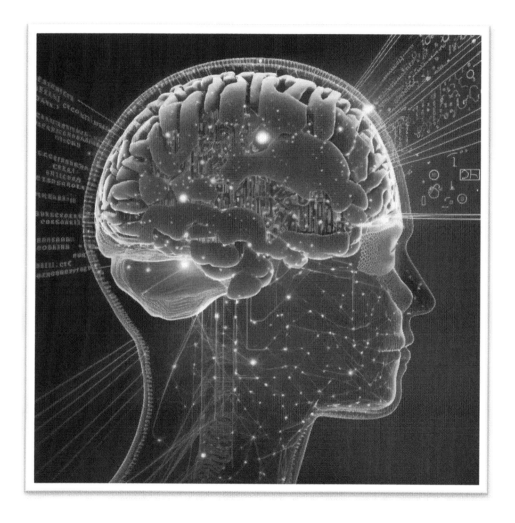

Mastery of the Mind

Becoming a Safe Person to Love

By Beth An Schulz, MNLP, MHt, EFTP, EMIP, CMSC, MTT

"The lotus is the most beautiful flower, whose petals open one by one. But it will only grow in the mud. In order to grow and gain wisdom, first you must have the mud — the obstacles of life and its suffering. ... The mud speaks of the common ground that humans share, no matter what our stations in life. ... Whether we have it all or we have nothing, we are all faced with the same obstacles: sadness, loss, illness, dying and death. If we are to strive as human beings to gain more wisdom, more kindness and more compassion, we must have the intention to grow as a lotus and open each petal one by one."–Goldie Hawn.

The journey of a lotus flower and the endeavor to become a safe person to love are intricately intertwined narratives of human growth, resilience, and vulnerability. The lotus flower starts its life journey in muddy, murky waters. Despite its surroundings, it strives towards the surface, seeking light and warmth.

As it grows, it gradually emerges from the depths, symbolizing purity, enlightenment, and spiritual awakening. Finally, it blossoms into a beautiful flower, representing beauty, resilience, and the journey from darkness to light.

Just as the lotus flower emerges from the depths of murky waters to bloom in radiant beauty, our own journeys often begin amidst the challenges and uncertainties of life. Similarly, like the layers of walls we construct around ourselves for protection, we often find solace in the safety of our emotional barriers, shielding ourselves from potential hurt and rejection, often as a response to past hurt or fears.

Yet, just as the lotus pushes through the mire to reach the surface, we too must confront and dismantle these barriers to embrace the richness of human connection. Removing these walls involves a process of introspection, self-awareness, and courage to dismantle the barriers we've built. It requires vulnerability and openness to let others in and connect, despite the risks.

In this journey, we strive not only to open ourselves to love but also to become a safe harbor for others—a sanctuary where vulnerability is embraced, and acceptance reigns supreme. Together, these analogies serve as poignant reminders of the transformative power of growth, resilience, and the courageous pursuit of authentic love and connection in our lives.

Let's delve deeper into the common themes of growth, resilience, and vulnerability as they relate to the journey of a lotus flower, building and removing walls, and becoming a safe person to love.

Growth:

The lotus flower's journey epitomizes growth, as it starts its life in the murky depths of the water and steadily reaches towards the light, blossoming into a radiant flower.

Similarly, building and removing walls represents growth on an emotional and psychological level. Building walls may initially offer a sense of safety, but true growth occurs when we confront and dismantle these barriers, allowing ourselves to experience genuine connections and intimacy.

Becoming a safe person to love also involves personal growth. It requires individuals to cultivate qualities such as empathy, patience, and understanding, which contribute to creating a nurturing environment for relationships to flourish.

Resilience:

The lotus flower shows resilience as it thrives in adverse conditions, pushing through the muddy waters to bloom. This resilience reflects the ability to persevere and flourish despite challenging circumstances.

Building and removing walls also require resilience. It takes courage to acknowledge and confront the reasons behind our self-imposed barriers, as well as resilience to navigate the vulnerability that comes with dismantling them.

Becoming a safe person to love demands resilience in the face of personal growth. It involves confronting our own insecurities and past traumas while remaining open to the vulnerabilities of others, all of which require inner strength and resilience.

Vulnerability:

Vulnerability is inherent in the journey of the lotus flower; it exposes itself to the elements as it grows towards the surface. This vulnerability is a necessary part of its transformation from a seed buried in mud to a beautiful flower.

Building and removing walls involves vulnerability. Building walls often stems from a fear of being hurt, while removing them requires the courage to be vulnerable and authentic in our interactions with others.

Becoming a safe person to love requires embracing vulnerability as a strength, rather than a weakness. It involves creating a space where individuals feel safe to express their true selves without fear of judgment or rejection, fostering deep and meaningful connections.

The analogies that have been described above share profound parallels in their symbolism and stages of growth. Now, let's explore these concepts further in our relationships and the pursuit of emotional safety.

Becoming a Safe Person to Love

Being a safe person to love means cultivating qualities, such as empathy, compassion, and trustworthiness. It involves actively listening, understanding, and validating the emotions and experiences of our loved ones.

A safe person creates a nurturing and supportive environment where others feel accepted, respected, and valued.

It requires continuous growth, self-reflection, and a willingness to confront and heal our own wounds to prevent projecting them onto others.

Exploring Emotional Safety in Relationships

In a world filled with uncertainties, one thing remains constant: the human desire for love and connection. However, amidst the pursuit of love, many find themselves tangled in relationships fraught with insecurities, fears, and doubts.

But what if there was a guide to becoming a safe person to love?

What if we could create relationships built on trust, respect, and emotional security?

This, my friends, is what we will explore.

By exploring the complexities of being a safe person to love, we must navigate the diverse landscapes of our relationships—from the bonds we share with family, to the connections we form with friends, and the intimate partnerships we cultivate romantically. Each relationship dynamic presents its own set of challenges and opportunities for growth, but the common thread that binds them all is the need for emotional safety.

Within our families, emotional safety lays the foundation for nurturing and supportive relationships. It provides a sanctuary where familial love can blossom, free from the constraints of judgment or rejection. In these sacred spaces, we learn the value of unconditional acceptance and the power of forgiveness, forging bonds that withstand the test of time.

Among friends, emotional safety fosters a sense of camaraderie and belonging. It creates an environment where authenticity thrives, allowing us to share our joys and sorrows, dreams, and fears, without fear of ridicule or betrayal. In these cherished friendships, we discover the beauty of mutual respect and unwavering loyalty, enriching our lives with shared experiences and cherished moments.

And in romantic partnerships, emotional safety is the cornerstone of lasting love and intimacy. It enables us to lower our walls and expose our vulnerabilities, knowing that our hearts are safe in the hands of our beloved. In these tender relationships, we experience the transformative power of trust and intimacy, weaving together our hopes and dreams into a montage of shared love and devotion.

In the exploration, we come to understand that being a safe person to love transcends mere words or action; it is a state of being deeply rooted in empathy, compassion, and authenticity. It requires us to confront our own insecurities and fears, to acknowledge the wounds of our past, and to heal them with gentleness and grace. Only then can we truly offer ourselves as a safe harbor for others, providing them with the sanctuary they need to thrive and flourish.

As we navigate the complexities of our relationships, we learn to cultivate the qualities of patience and understanding, recognizing that everyone carries their own burdens and struggles. We strive to be a source of strength and support, offering a listening ear and a compassionate heart to those in need. We honor their boundaries and respect their autonomy, allowing them the freedom to express themselves fully and authentically.

In the embrace of our love, others find solace and sanctuary, a refuge from the storms of life. They find acceptance and validation, knowing they are valued and cherished for who they are. They find encouragement and inspiration, as we empower them to pursue their dreams and aspirations. And most importantly, they find unconditional love, a love that knows no bounds and endures through all trials and tribulations.

As we journey together towards becoming safe people to love, we discover the profound joy and fulfillment that comes from giving ourselves to others. We experience the beauty of genuine connection and the transformative power of love, as it binds us in a series of shared experiences and shared hearts.

We realize that being a safe person to love is not just about the impact we have on others, but also about the transformation that occurs within ourselves. It is about becoming the best version of ourselves–kinder, more compassionate, and more loving–as we strive to create a world where love reigns supreme, and all who seek its embrace find solace in the warmth of our hearts.

In our quest to become safe havens for love, we embark on a profound journey of self-discovery and growth. We delve deep into the recesses of our hearts, confronting the shadows that lurk within and embracing the light that shines through. We learn to be gentle with ourselves, to offer ourselves the same compassion and understanding that we extend to others.

Navigating the Journey of Love and Growth

Through this journey, we come to recognize the interconnectedness of all beings, the inherent worth and dignity that resides within each soul. We understand that to love another is to see them not as distinct from ourselves, but as an integral part of the process of constructing life. And in honoring the sacredness of each individual, we honor the divine spark that lives within us all.

As we cultivate emotional safety within ourselves, we also become adept at nurturing it in our relationships. We learn to listen deeply, to hear not just the words spoken, but the emotions underlying them. We practice empathy and compassion, seeking to understand the experience and perspectives of those we love, without judgment and criticism.

In our interactions with others, we strive to create space for acceptance and validation, where vulnerability is celebrated rather than feared. We recognize it is through our shared vulnerabilities that true intimacy is forged, and we embrace the courage it takes to open our hearts to another.

But most importantly, we come to understand that being a safe person to love is an ongoing journey, a continuous process of growth and evolution. We acknowledge we will make mistakes along the way, that we will stumble and fall, but we also know that each misstep is an opportunity for learning and growing.

And so, my friends, with hearts open and spirits lifted, we embrace the path laid out before us, knowing that with each step we take, we draw closer to becoming the safe harbor for love that we aspire to be. For in the end, it is not the destination that matters, but the journey itself—the journey towards becoming the most authentic, compassionate, and loving versions of ourselves.

About Beth An Schulz, MNLP, MHt, EFTP, EMIP, CMSC, MTT

 In the ever-evolving world of life coaching, Beth An Schulz stands out as a dynamic force for guidance and transformation. Beth An, residing in sunny SWFL, brings a fresh perspective on the journey of personal self-discovery and growth. With a compassionate demeanor and a wealth of expertise, she emerges as a reliable ally for individuals navigating the unpredictable twists and turns of life.

As the visionary driving Tranquility Life Coaching, LLC, Beth An extends her caring hand to those bravely traversing life's tumultuous waters. Whether they're exploring the depths of self-discovery or weathering the storms of significant life transitions, Beth An's unwavering guidance serves as a steadfast beacon, guiding them toward clarity and fulfillment.

Beth An uses a diverse toolkit of modalities, including Neuro-Linguistic Programming (NLP), Hypnotherapy, Success Coaching, EFT, Breathwork, and TIME Techniques® to facilitate profound personal growth and transformation with her clients. Whether they're grappling with mid-life stresses, confronting major life decisions, breaking free from limiting beliefs or enacting positive changes in their lives, Beth An remains unwavering in her commitment to supporting them in achieving their goals and unlocking their fullest potential.

Get Beth An's free gift: www.mind-book.net/gift/Beth-An

Mastery of the Mind

Brain Hacks!
Simple Things for Extraordinary Results
By Dr. Heather Ingbretson

I was 12-years old when I learned about Helen Wolfgang. What happened to her changed the trajectory of my life. I will never forget it.

I ***can't*** ever forget it.

It has caused me unrelenting fear and the search for an answer—a solution to her problem—for my entire life. It was a fate worse than death in my mind. And I was determined to never let it happen to me or anybody that I loved!

Helen was a family friend who lived in West Virginia. Her home was a refuge from the oppressive Ohio Valley heat and humidity. Each summer, my family would pack up in our Volkswagen mini-van and travel from Minnesota to Woodsfield, Ohio. Woodsfield is a town of 2,000 people. It had grocery stores, a five and dime store, and a bank. Driving on towards Antioch, there is a little hairpin turn, and that is where we call home for 2 weeks every summer. The smell of Creeping Charlie filled the air and when the heat became unbearable, we planned a trip to see Helen and Earl, and their family.

They had Air Conditioning. And they had a TV, not that we could watch it but, we didn't care because they also had games!

Helen was always cooking or offering us food. I ate everything she would offer me. Helen and Earl were the refuge away from the heat, the pollen, the headaches, and bore of a house with no games, with no TV and nothing to do. Plus, Helen and Earl had KIDS and BONUS — they had OLDER kids. Older kids meant someone to look up to and show you the ropes and FUN and ADVENTURE.

So, Helen and Earl were a fixture in my family's conversation, and we often looked forward to our visits with them.

Then one year it all changed. The news arrived. Helen had a stroke. This time we would be visiting NOT as a social visit, but to see if we could somehow help. Earl greeted us at the door and Helen smiled her usual smile and shook hands or hugged us. What had changed was her now slightly crooked smile, and she was not speaking. One of her arms was weak. And at one point, she tried to tell Earl she didn't want the egg yolks in her egg salad because of the cholesterol, but she was deduced to grunting and pointing. The same happened with tying her shoes. She struggled with doing it one-handed, but she also couldn't ask for help. She had no words. No way to communicate.

It seemed, in my eyes, *a fate worse than death*! There was not much we could do to help, but our visit comforted Earl and the conversation was a brightness in his new journey.

However, the memories of her *struggling with communication* continued to haunt me for years.

I wondered what could be done, so that this didn't happen to ME or to my loved ones. I would spend the next 20 years pondering this question, only to find the answer in the most unlikely way.

Fast forward 20 years and I am in an advanced Neurology class with a colleague and working on a lady in a wheelchair. She also had lost the ability to speak and so her husband was doing the talking for her.

She had a stroke too, but hers is worse. Her legs are weak, and she is wheelchair bound. The professor is talking to the husband who describes her issues, and we are working on strengthening her brain-leg connection. The husband speaks with a charming accent. He's a sweet old man of 70s or 80s, perhaps. Hard to tell because it's clear he has had a hard life.

The professor asks, "Where did you and your wife meet?"

The man lifts his eyebrows and smiles- a simple question for him to answer. It brings back wonderful memories.

"Ah, we met in college *years ago*," he says, clearly reminiscing.

The professor nods, understanding. "And where was that?"

"Oh, Strasbourg. Back in Germany," he said, smiling and nodding. Memories together likely fill his mind.

"Do you speak any German at home?" the professor pressed on.

"No, never. We are here in America. We speak only English." This confused me a bit, but I could respect that.

"Would you do me a favor and ask your wife how she is today in German?"

"Ah. Sure." He turns to his wife and says, "Wie geht es dir heute, meine Liebe?"

Turning to him, her eyes become bright. She smiles, and she replies in perfect German, whatever was going on in her mind.

She was speaking, and this was a miracle!

There was not a dry eye in the crowd of Neurology students.

The class broke out in a million conversations.

"How did that happen?"

"How is she suddenly speaking?"

"I thought she lost her language skills."

"What just happened?"

The husband was crying now and embracing his wife. She was laughing, and the Professor leaned back with a big grin. This **was** a MIRACLE and YET, this was JUST Neurology.

This is one of mother nature's **brain hacks**. An insurance policy for communication. This is one of the best life lessons I ever learned.

When we learn to speak, our language is learned and stored on the LEFT temporal side of the brain. On the left just above the ear. And when we learn a 2nd or 3rd language, we learn it on the RIGHT side of the brain. Again, just above the ear or the RIGHT temporal lobe. When we learn a second language, we ensure we have divided and stored our ability to communicate in multiple areas of the brain. This is like diversification with financial investments.

IF one fails. We can fall back on the other!

I couldn't help Helen. She had long passed, but I could help myself and I could help my family. I could help all my future patients and, just maybe, I could help the world.

In the United States, where everyone knows English, there is little motivation to learn a second language.

However, I have made it my mission in life to let everyone know that learning a second language is your insurance policy to ensure that if you were to have damage to your brain, you WILL keep at least *one language*.

Learning a language is FREE. You can subscribe to Duolingo on your phone and learn one of dozens of languages of your choosing. It used to be expensive or difficult to hear a native speaker. With Duolingo, it is FREE and is as good or better than what you can get from a college course.

I should know, I took French in High school, and a year of French in college. Then I started Duolingo, and I began with Spanish because there are more Spanish speakers in

Minnesota. I am now fluent in Spanish and can get by in French. One interesting fact is that if you DO lose your primary language, you CAN re-learn your primary language on the other side of the brain—BUT you may find you end up with a bit of an accent. Charming, right?

So, luckily, my mom never ended up with a stroke. And that's good, because although her dad, Peter, spoke fluent French, he didn't speak it around the house. That might have been because Peter's wife didn't speak any French and Peter's mother didn't like his wife. So, Peter's mom would mumble under her breath in French about all the things and talk to Peter about the wife. Finally, the wife put her foot down.

"NO FRENCH IN THE HOUSE!"

And that is why the only phrases my mother ever learned are "Vite vite vite" (vee-duh vee-duh veet) or "Quickly, quickly, quickly" and "Venez manger"- (ven-AYE mah-zhay) or "come eat."

My mom is also very smart. She got her degree in engineering, just like my dad. She was one of the first female engineers in the state of MN and earned a full ride through college with straight A's.

However, there was another brain problem that was lurking in my mom that even as a child, I could see it beginning. Sometimes she couldn't find her words despite her incredible brain. And this from a strong woman who was what we call an *auditory processor*.

My mother LOVED to talk. This was her love language.

She loved to catch up, and she was ALWAYS up for the latest "gossip." If you wanted a brownie with her, you just needed to tell her **who said what**.

At the end of a long day, after supper was done, my sister and I had the chore to "clean up" after supper. Then my mom and dad would close the pocket door that slid closed between the living room and the kitchen so that they could "have tea and coffee" and download the day's happenings so my mom could get all the gossip. And at bedtime, my parents would sit and watch TV while having a bedtime snack.

My sister and I started seeing her struggling with her words as young kids. Then, as she got older, you could see the frustration as she would go through all the words and stammer, trying to find the word.

"Did you put the, uh, uh, uh" while she was pointing her finger, searching for the word.

…. The "CASSEROLE," she would finish. "Did you put the *casserole* in the oven?"

These instances started being increasingly common. Her body broke down, too. Her ankles were bad. She had a condition in her ankles that required her to get surgery when she was in her 20s. The foot doctor couldn't do much about it. Even now, as a chiropractor, there was not much to be done. Walking became difficult for her and then her brain deteriorated from there.

The mind and the body are connected. There is no doubt about it. Stop your body from moving and your mind will slow down. Your brain will get sluggish. The WORST thing to do is to stop moving. But that is another chapter in another book.

Here we are talking about things called "amyloid plaques."

Think of them as **road construction on the highway**. They need to be repaired, so you put cones around the lane. Well, that slows down the traffic or the ability for cars to use the lane. The brain has highways in it, too, and these amyloid plaques take up the lanes and slow down the signals until they get cleaned up.

Luckily, there is an enzyme that does this. It works **at night when we are sleeping**. But it has a PRIMARY job which is to clean up insulin. Insulin is a chemical that is released when our blood sugar is high. What is important is to understand is that **when you eat, you release INSULIN**.

So, if you eat right before bedtime, you are releasing INSULIN. And guess what? That enzyme that removes the road construction cones, which does the repair, stays too busy to finish cleaning up the road construction cones.

So, what is the fix? Once or twice a week, eat nothing for 2-3 hours before you go to sleep. Sounds easy, but I know it is difficult for everyone. We all like to eat while watching our shows, don't we? Or right before bed. So, what are we to do?

Drink tea or water, we only need to do this once or twice per week.

This would allow the amyloid plaques–the road construction cones — to be removed and to clear up our brain to function better. Better yet–do it for a week in a row and see how clearly you feel your brain becomes!

I challenge you to try this brain hack. Better yet.

For more free and accessible body, brain, and mental hacks, check out my free extras.

About Dr. Heather Ingbretson

 Dr. Heather Ingbretson, a seasoned chiropractor with 19 years of experience, holds a Doctorate from Northwestern Health Sciences University. Her primary focus is easing chronic pain and addressing brain injuries by identifying root causes and fortifying the body's resilience.

Recognized as a top chiropractor in Minnesota for five consecutive years, Heather's dedication to excellence extends to her practice in Roseville, where she has earned further accolades. At Ingbretson Chiropractic, Heather offers personalized treatment plans, delivering compassionate care tailored to each patient's needs.

Heather takes pride in enhancing her patients' quality of life and remains committed to ongoing education, staying abreast of the latest advancements in chiropractic care. Embracing a holistic approach to healing and wellness, she strives to empower her patients to achieve optimal health and vitality.

For those seeking relief from persistent health issues, Heather offers a unique gift: healing solutions beyond conventional treatments. Visit her practice to discover the difference firsthand.

Get Heather's free gift: www.mind-book.net/gift/Heather

Mastery of the Mind

Shaping Reality Through Thoughts

By Dean Afzal, CCHt, NLPP, PTT, CSC, EFT

Have you wondered how the stories you tell shape your life? Let's unravel the power of the mind and how your thoughts create the reality you live in. Most focus on the negatives, not realizing that your thoughts and emotions play puppeteer to the reality you experience. Imagine your mind as a unique universe, processing a staggering 2.3 million bits per second of information, but consciously grasping only 126. Your reality, based on where you focus those 128 bits, is uniquely yours. Intentions, focus, thoughts, and emotions are the architects of your destiny, making it vital to steer your attention toward what you want rather than what you fear.

So, if you want to make the most of your thoughts to reach your goals, like being healthy, successful in your job or business, or building wealth, it's important to control negative thoughts and turn them into positive ones. When you replace a negative thought with a positive one, it's a little victory. And the more you do it, the easier it becomes to think positively. Let's go through some examples and see how you can use this in your daily life.

Visualizing Success: Targeting Systems and Labels

Have you ever noticed that once you buy a new car, you see it everywhere? It's like your brain switches on a special radar, similar to what fighter jets use, called your reticular activating system. When you focus on specific goals for success or health, it's like you're opening new opportunities that you didn't notice before, changing how you see the world around you. Wouldn't you rather focus on what you want instead of what you're trying to avoid?

Now, let's talk about the negative side of this idea - labeling yourself or others. When you give someone a label, like "introvert", "lazy", or "ADHD", it puts them in a box and tells them how they should think, act, and feel. Labels are common, but they're harmful because they limit you and give you permission to only act within those limits. Remember, what you think about and focus on becomes your reality, whether you realize it. So, it's important not to label anyone, including yourself, and not to let others do it to you. Especially with children!

Now that you've explored the significance of your thoughts, let's discuss perspective - the power to change your life just by looking at things differently. Let's dive into that next.

Breaking Through Stagnation by Reframing Perspective

Picture hitting a wall and feeling stuck. You may stay stuck, blaming everything and everyone, or you may turn it into rocket fuel, propelling yourself forward and uplifting those around you. In my two-decade career journey from high-tech startups to corporate America and entrepreneurship, navigating obstacles was perpetual. Getting stuck and not knowing what direction to take would be constant and keep coming up repeatedly. Whether it was taking a new product

The Pathway to Empowerment

to market or taking an existing product into new markets, building a new team, or upskilling an existing team, crafting a new go-to-market strategy, or boosting sales with an existing customer base–the question is, what do you do when you get stuck?

Getting unstuck is simple yet elusive when deep in the spiral of the same problem and emotional state. It's like trying to read a label inside a jar or thinking outside the box while inside it. The key is to change perspective, *reframe the problem*, and ask the right questions. Let's explore how to do this in various scenarios.

Reframing Career Focus

When you first graduate from college, you may think about putting in a lot of effort to get noticed and grow in your job. But it's important to change how you see things. Instead of just thinking about how much time you're spending, focus on what you're achieving. Think about the results that make a difference, like helping the company grow, improving its reputation, bringing in new talented people, or clearing up misunderstandings between different parts of the company. It's about focusing on the goals that matter and can make a big impact.

In the early years of my career, the allure of working long hours was undeniable. However, a mentor's advice reshaped my perspective. Instead of fixating on hours clocked, I redirected my efforts toward impactful contributions. This shift not only sped up my professional growth, but also influenced a cultural shift within the workplace. Successive promotions, I realized, were not merely a byproduct of hard work but a result of aligning efforts with meaningful contributions that resonated with the company's objectives.

Reframing Management Empathy and Connection

Many bosses think that because they've worked hard and reached a certain position, they should be able to tell others what to do. They believe that since they had to go through tough times, everyone else should, too. But this way of thinking is self-centered.

A better way to frame leadership, which is what outstanding leaders do, is to care genuinely about your team members' health, happiness, and personal development on a human level. Take the time to understand what your team members are going through — their struggles, worries, hopes, what motivates them, and what they're good at and not so good at. Then, do everything you can to help them.

When you understand and support your team members' growth, something magical happens. The team members go above and beyond because they want to, not just because they must. A simple change in perspective makes a vast difference, and employees can feel it.

Reframing Business Abundance Mindset

In the business world, a major "aha" moment and shift in perspective comes when you realize that there's enough success for everyone. Instead of obsessing over your competitors, it's better to focus on what makes you unique and what you do best. This brings more joy and energy to your work.

Many entrepreneurs spend too much time worrying about what competitors are doing. But this drains your happiness and motivation. A better approach is to concentrate on your strengths and what sets your product or service apart. Different people like different things, so it's okay if some customers prefer your competitors.

Another important mindset shift is to enjoy the journey of growth, rather than rushing to reach your goals as quickly as possible, no matter the cost of time, stress, or strained relationships. When you take pleasure in the process, success naturally follows.

New businesses often want to go from making a little money to making millions overnight. But it's better to focus on reaching smaller goals first, then scaling up. Celebrate each minor success along the way, set milestone goals that are challenging but achievable, and keep believing that there's plenty of success to go around. This positive mindset leads to lasting success.

Reframing Personal Discomfort

Have you ever been stuck in traffic? Instead of feeling frustrated, try setting a goal to learn something new before you reach your destination. For instance, you could listen to a podcast or an audiobook. This way, the time passes more quickly because you're focused on achieving your learning goal.

In my personal life, I've learned to see discomfort as a sign of growth. So, when I'm feeling uncomfortable and have a lot going on at once, like working on a new investment project, dealing with changes in my business, and managing family commitments, I remind myself that these challenges mean I'm growing. This mindset helps me stay positive and manage my time and energy more effectively. It also encourages me to delegate tasks and helps my team develop new skills, so they can share the workload.

By seeing discomfort as an opportunity for growth, juggling multiple tasks becomes exciting rather than overwhelming.

You've read how your thoughts and perspectives can shape your life. Now, let's discuss how to make positive changes easily by living in the moment, embracing uncertainty, and tapping into its power.

Living in the Now: Embracing the Present

You've probably heard a lot about being present and living in the moment, but what does that mean? It's about letting go of the past and not worrying about the future. Unfortunately, many spend too much time dwelling on what's already happened or what might happen later. When you focus too much on the past or the future, you're trying to control everything instead of embracing the possibilities of the present moment. Your expectations of the future are based on your experiences, which can discourage if those experiences weren't great.

Here's a simple exercise to try: Close your eyes, take a few deep breaths, and pay attention to your surroundings. Feel the chair beneath you, notice the sensation of your feet on the ground, listen to the surrounding sounds you hadn't noticed before, and feel any tension in your body releasing with each breath. Try to stay in this moment for a few minutes without thinking about anything from the past or future.

How do you feel? Pretty amazing, right? There's so much beauty and richness in life that we often overlook. Even just spending a moment with someone you care about, saying nothing, can bring so much joy and appreciation.

Living in the present moment is also where you'll find the best ideas and inspiration. They seem to come to you effortlessly. For example, my brothers and I love hiking together, and we take on a challenge every year. Last year, we climbed Mount Kilimanjaro, the tallest free-standing mountain in Africa, with a summit of 19,431 feet. We invited three close friends to join us, which was a first for us. We opted for one of the tougher trails and planned to complete the climb in seven days.

During the journey, I noticed something interesting about one of my friends. At the end of each day's climb, when we gathered for dinner, he would start worrying about the next day and all the things that could go wrong. It brought down the energy of the group and took away from the joy of celebrating our achievements. I spoke to him about it, and he realized that he was doing the same thing in his everyday life, robbing himself of happiness by focusing on things that might never happen.

The same goes for dwelling on the past, thinking about what you could have done differently. What's done is done. Learn from it, grow, and move forward, knowing that you're stronger because of your experiences.

Brighter Than Before

You have the power to shape your own reality. How amazing is that? Bringing it all together, it all begins with controlling your thoughts, concentrating on what you desire instead of what you fear, refusing to accept negative labels or past burdens, looking at problems as chances to grow, and enjoying the present moment. This is the secret to a satisfying and meaningful life, crafted by none other than yourself! Your mind is like a magic wand; you just need to use it wisely and witness your reality change before your eyes.

About Dean Afzal, CCHt, NLPP, PTT, CSC, EFT

Dean Afzal is a highly accomplished professional with over 25 years of expertise in business strategy, marketing, and leadership. He holds a Bachelor of Science degree in Mathematics, Statistics, Economics, Marketing, and Management from DePaul University and certifications in Neurolinguistic Programming, Hypnotherapy, Time Techniques, EFT, and Life and Success Coaching from Transform Destiny.

As the President of Puresome Group, Dean specializes in helping Startup Founders, Leaders at Fortune 500 Companies, and forward-thinking CXOs develop growth-focused GTM strategies, increase revenue through integrated marketing programs, and create customer-centered product roadmaps.

His dedication to excellence and innovation has earned him numerous awards and recognition, including becoming an honorary member of the Delta Mu Delta Honor Society, highlighting his commitment to academic achievement and leadership in the business community.

Dean Afzal is a trusted advisor and mentor to business professionals seeking to drive growth, increase profitability, and make a lasting impact on their industries.

Get Dean's free gift: www.mind-book.net/gift/Dean

Mastery of the Mind

Empower Your Essence
Mastering the Mindset Journey
By Rahila Ali, CCHt, NLPP, PTT, CSC, EFT

Within our minds' expansive terrain lies an untapped potential awaiting liberation—a reservoir too often overlooked until catalyzed by significant and often traumatic events. I learned this truth the hard way. Fourteen years ago, I was living a happy life with two young children and a loving husband when I was given a year and a half to live. I felt sad, depressed, and lifeless, with no hope. Dealing with illness and being on my deathbed several times, I saw myself merely hanging on threads of life that could have been broken at any time.

Placed on a regime of immunosuppressants, I felt the steady descent of my health. I was incapable of tending to my children, managing the household, or fulfilling even the simplest of tasks. I had thoughts I'd be at peace once my soul left this sick body.

Amidst the haze of illness, a realization pierced through my consciousness like a shard of glass: in my absence, who would shower my children with boundless affection and care only a mother could provide?

Watching my three-year-old daughter take care of her 18-month-old sibling shattered my heart into a thousand pieces. Instead of reveling in the joys of childhood with dolls and embracing imaginary companions, she found herself immersed in a world of make-believe appointments, dialing toy phones with a solemnity far beyond her tender years. "Is this Dr. So-and-So's office?" her innocent voice rang out, a stark reminder of the burden she carried in my stead.

Meanwhile, my son, yearning for the embrace of his mother, encountered only the cruel reality of my physical frailty. His outstretched arms, craving the warmth of my touch, found no solace in my weakened grasp. The agony of his longing, coupled with the bitter sting of illness that kept us apart, seared into my soul with an intensity that defied description.

What kind of childhood memories were being made? The question gnawed at my spirit, shaking me to the core of my being. It was then, in despair, that a fierce determination ignited within me- a resolve to wrestle back control from the clutches of sickness, reclaim my role as a mother, and reshape the narrative of our shared existence.

Little did I know back then. I started to explore and understand our state of being, how our physical body works, and our mental state. Depths of our beliefs and thoughts and the incredible power we possess within. I embarked on a journey to understand our mindset and master it.

The Foundations of Mindset

Our mindset, the lens through which we perceive the world, is shaped by our beliefs and attitudes. Here, we delve into the foundational elements that make up our mindset—

examining the impact of our beliefs on our actions and outcomes.

As I was going through my treatments, the doctors kept switching the diagnosis, keeping me puzzled by what was going on. I kept my hopes high as I wanted to feel better and wanted my bloodwork to be normal, hoping all this was a mistake. Hoping this was a dream and a bad one, I'd wake up, and everything would return to normal.

One day, my doctor sat me down and told me, "Rahila, you need to understand you're sick. Your life will never be the same. Forget about all your dreams and just focus on whatever time you have left with loved ones. You can't live like you used to and must be vigilant about everything."

Those words just shattered all my hopes and dreams. A million thoughts raced through my mind, thinking about my family and what they would go through; my husband, siblings, and children, whom I'd never be able to see grow, will miss their birthdays, graduation, weddings, and grandchildren. Even though I had never thought about those things, all of this gave me chills.

It felt like a freezing cold current went through my body, changing my identity. I'm a "sick person waiting to die." That's what I felt like while thinking about this day in and day out. Watching my kids play and they not knowing what's going on.

Maintaining a smile was crucial so that they wouldn't sense the depth of my struggles. Lacking the strength to share the doctor's prognosis with my family, I couldn't bear the thought of adding to their anguish. Not a word passed to my husband about the verdict I had received. Preserving our last moments together as joyful memories outweighed any inclination to burden him with sorrow.

Challenging Limiting Beliefs

Limiting beliefs function as unseen obstacles, impeding our progress. There is a process to identify and challenge these beliefs. By questioning the validity of our self-imposed constraints, we pave the way for a more expansive and empowering mindset.

As I internalized the label that was given to me. My life changed. I acted like my label. It was devastating and daunting on its own, but every action I took was based on this new perceived label and identity. The Identity that was never familiar, not feeling like myself, nothing made me happy. I spent days and nights just waiting for the time to pass.

This new feeling wasn't right in my heart, and something inside me wanted to change all this. One day, something came to my heart while I was praying. I remember this quote I heard while growing up: "Every disease has a cure except old age and death." Praying to God, day in and day out, I pleaded, "God, please help me, and if you help me, I will help others heal as well."

I needed to find this cure, so I started doing my research. I cleaned my diet and started doing some detox therapies. My results started getting better. The doctors couldn't believe the numbers from my test results. They asked me what I was doing. They laughed at me and told me these things didn't work, but guess what, it was working. My results kept improving, and soon I had the energy to get back on my feet. I started doing little chores around the house and caring for my children. My life was almost becoming normal.

The Power of Resilience

Resilience is the cornerstone of mindset mastery. Learn how to view challenges as opportunities for growth and develop the resilience needed to navigate life's twists and turns.

As things turned around, I felt better, but I still wouldn't feel good on some days. When I didn't feel good, things would go south again. It felt like I was stuck in a loop. I was doing all the right things to fix my physiology. Still, something wasn't working until I met this Holistic doctor whose prescription for me was, "Stay happy, think happy thoughts, and do some artwork."

I didn't quite understand him at first and left his office a little upset that he didn't give me any supplements or a magical holistic pill to pop that would fix everything. I was so focused on the physical that I forgot the importance of the mental. So, I started thinking about this and tried implementing what was prescribed. It made sense. Little did I know then that my thoughts also impacted my physical health.

Whenever I thought about my timeline, I unleashed a beast in my body that destroyed everything I built. That beast is called cortisol. Our thoughts have a direct impact on our physical being. Negative thoughts can make us sick, but positive thoughts can also improve our health. This was the most profound shift I had that day. I realized I changed my diet and lifestyle but had not changed my beliefs.

Nurturing a Growth Mindset

A growth mindset is the key to continuous improvement. Discover strategies to cultivate this mindset, embracing challenges with enthusiasm, and viewing failures as steppingstones to success. Uncover the transformative power of adopting a mindset focused on learning and development.

I discovered the biggest flaw in my strategies for attaining good health. I had to make sure that I was keeping a check on it as well. The root cause of the problem was not changing my mindset. I was so focused on the physical aspects of my health that I forgot the mental aspects. How does our mind keep running these programs on auto? No program can run smoothly until we change or eliminate the virus. In my subconscious, my mind was running a program that was still corrupt. It didn't match my actions and impacted my progress.

I had to go inside and change my identity, not live this label. I had to be me again. Once I made those changes, my life improved. Even though we sometimes forget our needs that are not visible, keeping a check on our mindset is the most important thing ever in life. Whether it's health, wellness, business, or family life, we must keep our mindsets in check. How we perceive things and how we project things are two different mechanisms.

Harnessing Perception's Power

As we conclude our journey to mastering the mind's terrain, remember this is an ongoing process. My journey toward healing began with a shift in mindset. As I challenged the limiting beliefs that had imprisoned me, I discovered the power of resilience and the transformative potential of a growth mindset. But it wasn't until I acknowledged the profound impact of my thoughts on my physical health that true progress was made.

As I embarked on a journey of self-discovery, I realized the root cause of my struggles lay not only in my body, but in my mind. By changing my beliefs, by refusing to accept the label of "sick," I reclaimed my identity and unlocked the path to healing.

As I stand here today, I am a testament to the power of perception and projection. By harnessing the power within, by reshaping my perception of the world around me, I have transformed my life and inspired others to embark on their own journey to mindset mastery.

Remember, dear reader, that this journey is ongoing. The power within you is vast and ever evolving. By unleashing this power, you can transform your life and inspire others to do the same. Embrace the journey, challenge your beliefs, and never underestimate the power of your own mind. For it is within the depths of your own consciousness that true liberation lies.

About Rahila Ali, CCHt, NLPP, PTT, CSC, EFT

 Rahila Ali is an experienced Wellness Coach with over 8 years in the health & wellness industry. A graduate of the BodyMind Institute and certified Raw Nutritionist, she also holds certifications in NLP, Hypnotherapy, EFT, Success, and Life Coaching from Transform Destiny.

Rahila empowers clients to shift their mindset from victim to victor, helping them achieve wellness goals and live their best lives.

Recognized as a top coach in Chicago, Rahila has been a guest speaker on many shows and featured in NY Weekly and a documentary for her impactful work.

Dedicated to making a positive impact, Rahila's holistic approach and commitment to empowerment offer valuable support to those seeking transformation.

Get Rahila's free gift: www.mind-book.net/gift/Rahila

Mastery of the Mind

Ignite Growth in Yourself
and Inspire Transformation in Others
By Jerry Valerio, CCHt, NLPP, PTT, CSC, EFT

Journey of a Thousand Miles

Laozi's ancient Chinese proverb, "A journey of a thousand miles begins with a single step," captures the essence of personal growth and transformation. Just as a journey unfolds through successive steps, transformation involves a continuous process of actions and choices that propel us toward our fullest potential. While the idea of an instant, sweeping change (like the snap of a finger or the granting of a magical genie bottle wish) can be alluring, true growth often unfolds in smaller increments, requiring consistent effort and sometimes even the courage to change course.

Transformation begins with self-awareness, which is the bedrock of sustainable growth. By fostering a deep understanding of our aspirations, core values, strengths, and weaknesses, we gain the clarity to chart a meaningful life path. This self-knowledge empowers us to set goals aligned with our true selves, ensuring our direction is intentional and purposeful.

Challenges are an inevitable part of our growth journey. A growth mindset, which sees obstacles as opportunities to learn and adapt, is essential for progress. Resilience, overcoming setbacks, and maintaining optimism keep us moving forward. Equally important is grit - the unwavering passion and perseverance to pursue our long-term goals, motivating us to stay on course in the face of difficulties.

The pursuit of knowledge should go beyond formal education. In our ever-changing world, lifelong learning is paramount. Embracing a curious spirit and actively seeking diverse learning experiences through engaging with the world, mentorships, online courses (e.g., Coursera, Gaia, Masterclass, Mindvalley), travel, and workshops-enables ongoing personal and intellectual expansion.

Finally, personal growth is not solely about individual gain. As we evolve, our determination and progress can inspire and uplift those around us, creating positive ripple effects throughout our communities. Let's explore the elements that spark personal growth, offering strategies to overcome challenges, fuel a thirst for knowledge, and empower ourselves and others to strive for self-improvement.

Igniting Growth | Inner Exploration

The seeds of transformation lie within. Inner exploration-the intentional practice of turning awareness inward-allows these seeds to sprout and flourish. Self-awareness is the key that unlocks potential, guides through challenges, and empowers us to live in alignment with values and aspirations.

Here are potent tools to embark on this exploration:

- Journaling: Let our journal become a sanctuary for our minds. Let our thoughts flow onto the page, unraveling emotions, identifying patterns, and celebrating your growth journey.

- Meditation: Cultivate mindfulness, the art of observing our thoughts and feelings without judgment. Through stillness, we can access deeper layers of ourselves and discover aspects beneath the surface.

- Personality Assessments: Tools like the Core Values Index Assessment, Myers-Briggs Type Indicator, or the Enneagram offer frameworks to understand our motivations, strengths, and tendencies. While these shouldn't define us, they can illuminate unrecognized aspects of our personalities.

- SMART Goal setting: Goals are our guiding stars. The SMART framework (Specific, Measurable, Achievable, Relevant, and Time-bound) ensures our goals are focused and actionable. True power comes from aligning our goals with the self-understanding we've gained through inner exploration, which ignites authentic growth.

Tip: Breathwork as a form of meditation and mindfulness is a powerful wellness tool for coping with life's stressors. It can elevate mood. The simplest breathwork is box breathing – inhale deeply for 4-seconds, hold for 4-seconds, exhale completely for 4-seconds, hold for 4-seconds, and repeat over 10-15 minutes or longer.

This is a journey, not a race. Be patient and kind with yourself and celebrate each step toward a deeper understanding of the remarkable person you are.

Igniting Growth | Embracing Challenges

Life's journey comes with challenges. How we respond to them shapes our personal growth. We can shrink from them, let them dim our potential, or embrace them as the catalysts they are - opportunities to become more capable, stronger, and wiser.

The first step is cultivating a growth mindset. This outlook changes our relationship with setbacks. Instead of seeing limitations, we believe our abilities can evolve through effort and experience. When a problem arises, a growth mindset asks: "What can I learn from this? How can I approach it differently?"

To navigate challenges, resilience is vital. It's the ability to bounce back from hardship, to adapt, and to stay hopeful even when things are tough. Build resilience by practicing mindfulness to manage stress, replacing negative self-talk with positive affirmations, and leaning on a support network of family, friends, or professionals for guidance.

Alongside resilience, grit gives us staying power. The fire inside keeps us striving for long-term goals, even when the way is hard. We fuel that fire by remembering why our goals matter, celebrating small wins, and recognizing that challenges often precede our most significant breakthroughs.

Embracing challenges doesn't mean being tough. Self-compassion is essential. We should treat ourselves with kindness, just like we would offer a friend. Understand that missteps along the way are part of the process.

Think of the significant figures in history: Nelson Mandela, imprisoned for fighting injustice yet using that experience to forge a more unified South Africa, and Marie Curie, who faced constant skepticism yet revolutionized science through her persistence. Their stories remind us that challenges are often the crucibles where our greatest potential is forged.

Igniting Growth | Lifelong Learning

Tip: Want to learn how to push beyond a comfort zone? Take on a fear and confront it directly. I had a fear of heights as a kid. Rollercoaster rides made me feel anxious. As an adult, I went tandem skydiving. I leaped and the net appeared or in my case, the parachute. Now I love the thrill of rollercoaster rides without any angst and anxiety. Feel the fear and do it anyway. It's amazing to do something that moves beyond fear and feeling frozen.

The joy of learning continues beyond a diploma. Embracing lifelong learning is a superpower that unlocks our potential, keeps our minds agile, and fuels our passions throughout life.

Think beyond classrooms and textbooks. The world is our learning laboratory! Online courses, webinars, and workshops put knowledge at our fingertips, from career skills to intriguing hobbies. Conferences connect us with experts and spark new ideas. Travel immerses us in different cultures, shattering assumptions and broadening our worldview.

Curiousness is the engine of lifelong learning. Ask questions, explore the unfamiliar, and see the world with the wonder of a child. Seek people with different perspectives-these conversations will stretch and enrich us. Volunteer to discover new challenges and potential passions.

Lifelong learning benefits more than just ourselves. Avid learners become adaptable problem-solvers, bringing fresh ideas to their communities and workplaces. A society that values continuous learning is dynamic and ready for whatever the future brings.

Inspiring Transformation | the Power of Influence

Always remember how our growth can ignite growth in others. While mentorship and encouragement are essential, our simple dedication to self-improvement can be a powerful, unspoken motivator. Transformation is contagious. - as people see us evolving, they believe in their potential for change.

Authenticity is key. If we preach lifelong learning, let our actions prove it - seek knowledge and build new skills. If we promote resilience, face challenges with determination and a positive outlook. We build trust and respect when we live out the values we hope to inspire. Personal assessments like the Core Values Index can help surface the core values that matter.

Our growth can create a ripple effect. Inspired, someone might kick start their journey and then inspire others. This shows the power of a community united in self-improvement: collaboration, progress, and boundless encouragement.

Think of the teacher whose passion for discovery makes students lifelong learners or the leader whose resilience in hardship inspires courage in their team. These are examples of everyday people whose transformative journeys affect countless lives.

True influence isn't about persuasion. It's about living our values and being the change we wish to see in the world. Our example can spark a fire in those around us.

Inspiring Transformation | Encouragement and Support

Leading by example is powerful, but to ignite growth in others means to offer active encouragement and support. It's the fuel that empowers people to reach their potential.

Positive reinforcement works wonders. Celebrate every step forward, big or small. This builds confidence and the desire to keep striving. Don't just praise results - applaud the effort, milestones reached, and the courage to keep going. By showing belief in someone's abilities, we nurture that belief within themselves.

Offer constructive feedback alongside encouragement. The key is a supportive, growth-focused approach. Frame feedback to tackle challenges and learn together. See setbacks as steppingstones instead of failures.

Active listening and affirmation are invaluable. Deep listening creates a safe space to share hopes and fears. Ask questions, express empathy, and reflect on what's heard to show understanding. This builds trust and a sense of being valued. Express genuine belief in the person's abilities, highlight their strengths, and offer support. - it can transform their self-belief and motivate them to persevere.

Tip: To truly foster growth in others, provide consistent and positive encouragement and support that celebrates effort, demonstrates genuine belief in their potential, is personalized, and offers constructive guidance. People do their best when they feel the love and support of "cheer" leaders in their camp.

Remember, everyone grows at their own pace. Tailor support to their unique needs and where they are on the path. This kind of personalized encouragement is the most meaningful and effective.

Growth and Transformation as a Way of Life

Igniting growth isn't just about bettering ourselves - it's a way to live more fully, connect deeply with our true selves, and uplift those around us. Transformation is both personal and communal:

- *Ignite Potential*: Cultivate curiosity, an unending thirst for knowledge, and an open heart. Embrace challenges, for they shape us. True growth means finding joy and strength in the ongoing evolution of mind, heart, and spirit.
- *Inspire Others*: Be authentic. Model resilience, celebrating effort, and offer unwavering support. When leading by example, we spark transformation in those around us - and their growth fuels us.

This journey has no end. Celebrate every victory, big and small. Notice the daily shifts in thoughts, feelings, and actions - this is transformation in motion.

Call to Action: The journey begins with a single step, but true growth means always moving forward.

Live life as if the best is yet to come always and in all ways.

Let's Grow Together - Forward, Onward, and Upward!

About Jerry Valerio, CCHt, NLPP, PTT, CSC, EFT

 Jerry Valerio is a Business, Career, and Life Coach dedicated to helping aspiring career professionals and entrepreneurs achieve their dreams and goals. Jerry brings a unique perspective to his coaching practice, drawing on his two-decades of business management, executive leadership, and sales career in the technology sector at both start-ups and scale-ups.

With inner work and mindset transformation and a focus on empowerment and growth, coach Jerry guides and ignites inspired individuals towards unleashing their full potential, unlocking infinite possibilities, and realizing their dreams. His heart-centered, human-connected passion for helping others makes him a compassionate and empathetic coach, committed to seeing his client's level up and succeed in life.

He also embraces the pursuit of thrilling experiences like auditioning for the reality TV show the Apprentice; tandem skydiving above the farmlands outside of Chicago; and zip lining down a Maui mountainside near Lahaina. Y-O-L-O.

Visit jerryvalerio.com to learn more about his coaching services and how he can help you on your journey to success.

Get Jerry's free gift: www.mind-book.net/gift/Jerry

Mastery of the Mind

Beyond Mindset
Embracing the Symphony of Mind, Body, and Spirit
By Dr. Laurie Emery

In the realm of personal development, the concept of mindset has assumed a central role, championed as the keystone for achieving success, happiness, and self-improvement. This emphasis on mindset — the set of attitudes or beliefs that shape how we interpret and respond to the world — is underpinned by a powerful truth: our thoughts profoundly influence our actions and our life's trajectory. Books, seminars, and coaching programs tout the transformational power of adopting a positive, growth-oriented mindset, arguing that with the right mental framework, any obstacle can be overcome, and any goal achieved.

However, while cultivating a resilient and positive mindset is beneficial, this focus presents a critical oversight. It suggests that by adjusting our thoughts and attitudes, we can navigate life's complexities and achieve a state of complete healing, empowerment, and fulfillment. This perspective, though well-intentioned, is akin to a gardener who tends to only the most visible parts of the plants while neglecting the roots and soil that provide nourishment and stability. Just as plants require a holistic approach to thrive, so too do human beings need more than mental fortitude to live actualized lives.

The Critical Role of Self-Connection

At the heart of true healing lies the critical task of connecting to oneself. It's not enough to understand our thoughts; we must also learn how to interpret the language of our bodies and emotions. Emotional energy, when not properly processed, becomes trapped within us.

This unprocessed energy can manifest as physical symptoms, such as chronic pain or tension, or psychological symptoms, including anxiety and depression. But the impact goes even deeper, affecting our ability to achieve our goals and live the life we desire.

For instance, consider someone striving for ideal health but unable to maintain habits that support their well-being. The root of this struggle may not be a lack of knowledge or discipline, but unprocessed emotional energy related to self-worth or fear of failure. Similarly, barriers to financial success often stem from deeper beliefs about money or self-value, encoded in our emotional energy from experiences. These beliefs act like invisible shackles, limiting our potential and sabotaging our efforts.

In the realm of career advancement, unprocessed emotions can create a ceiling we can't seem to break through. Doubts, fears, and unresolved past disappointments can lead to self-sabotaging behaviors or a lack of assertiveness, preventing us from reaching our full professional potential.

Relationships, too, are deeply impacted. Patterns of disconnection, divorce, or the pain of loneliness can often be traced back to trapped emotional energies of fear, abandonment, or unworthiness. Without processing these emotions, we may unknowingly repeat patterns that keep us from forming or sustaining meaningful connections.

This trapped energy not only holds us back from achieving specific outcomes like health, wealth, career success, and fulfilling relationships, but also from realizing our broader potential and living a fulfilled life. Connecting with and processing this emotional energy is, therefore, not just an act of healing; it's a pathway to unlocking our deepest aspirations and achieving our most cherished goals.

Unfulfilled Despite Mastery of Mindset

Consider the stories of high achievers who have mastered the art of positive thinking and goal setting: the executive who climbs the corporate ladder but struggles with chronic stress and a lack of meaningful relationships; the artist who achieves fame but battles with addiction and a sense of isolation; the athlete who pushes their body to its limits but feels lost upon retirement. These individuals may have cultivated powerful mindsets that drove their success, but their stories reveal a common theme of unfulfillment. Their mental resilience and focus brought them external achievements, yet internally, they encountered voids that mindset alone could not fill.

Somatic Processes: Embracing Every Part

The somatic approach to healing offers us a deeply transformative journey—one that requires us to tenderly embrace every aspect of our being with heartfelt dedication. This path is not merely about acknowledging the existence of our emotions and physical sensations; it's about delving into their profound depths, understanding their narratives, and honoring the wisdom they encapsulate.

At its essence, this approach champions the intricate connection between our bodies and emotions, each holding keys to our well-being and healing. Emotions manifest physically, creating sensations that narrate our internal experiences—a knot in the stomach signaling apprehension, the heat in our cheeks during embarrassment, or the heavy shoulders burdened by stress. These are the body's dialog, conveying crucial insights about our emotional landscape.

However, without a deep, introspective understanding of these signals, vital parts of us remain in the shadows, residing in our blind spots. For instance, the persistent tension in one's neck might not only signify physical strain, but could also reflect anxiety. To move beyond reacting to our emotions, we must develop the ability to process them— feeling and releasing them. This process is facilitated by what we refer to as the "5 Awarenesses," which guide us through identifying the origin of our thoughts and emotions in the body, understanding their nature, and allowing ourselves to experience and learn from them without resistance, repressed anger, or the weight of excessive responsibilities. Recognizing and accepting such signals not as mere inconveniences but as significant messages from our body, we start to uncover and address the underlying emotions and needs.

This journey goes beyond symptom management; it's an embrace of our complete selves. It involves cultivating a compassionate internal space that welcomes all parts of our existence, especially those we've neglected or suppressed. These unacknowledged parts—fear from past traumas, vulnerabilities shrouded in shame, or dreams deferred because of doubt—live in our blind spots, subtly steering our lives.

For those who repeatedly fall short of their goals, or achieving them only to stumble again, this lack of deep self-knowledge could be the culprit. Our unexplored emotions and sensations hold the power to influence our decisions, behaviors, and our life's trajectory. By neglecting to engage in a loving dialog with these parts of ourselves, we miss the opportunity to realign our actions with our deepest desires and needs.

Embracing the somatic approach means developing a new, harmonious relationship with ourselves—one where emotions and physical sensations are not obstacles but guides toward healing and wholeness. It teaches us to approach life's challenges with resilience, compassion, and a deeper understanding, transforming our relationship with ourselves and paving the way for true fulfillment and success.

The beauty of this journey lies in its ability to unveil the hidden parts of us, offering a path to a richer, more connected experience of life. By integrating these shadowed aspects into our conscious self, we unlock a level of self-awareness and empowerment.

Life Experiences

From a young age, we develop survival techniques to navigate our environment with the least amount of distress. These techniques, while protective, can hinder our growth and healing if they remain unexamined and unprocessed. They lead to forming beliefs and decisions that, though designed to keep us safe, keep us stuck in patterns that no longer serve us.

Reconnecting to Ourselves

The beliefs and decisions formed in early childhood have a profound impact on our adult lives. They shape our relationships, our financial situations, and our health. Without reconnecting and processing these early parts of ourselves, we continue to recreate the same undesired outcomes. Reconnecting with ourselves involves engaging in practices that allow us to explore and understand our bodily sensations and emotions. Through such somatic processes, we can release trapped energy, heal old wounds, and open pathways to new ways of being and relating.

Integrating New Pathways for Healing

The somatic approach to healing invites us into a deeply transformative journey, one that not only asks us to tenderly embrace every aspect of our being, but also to recognize our existence as spiritual beings having a human experience. This profound perspective illuminates the necessity of engaging with the human condition—our minds, our emotions, and our physical sensations—not as mere biological phenomena but as vital messages guiding us toward what seeks to be seen, felt, and deeply understood.

Within this framework, our emotions and bodily sensations are not random or meaningless; they are direct communications from our deeper selves, signposts pointing us towards areas of our lives that require attention and healing. However, without acknowledging and integrating these signals into our conscious awareness, we risk remaining within the confines of a safe and comfortable box, one that may yield certain results and levels of success but restricts us from embracing the extraordinary life we can create.

This is where the spiritual dimension of our existence becomes crucial. Our "unfinished stuff"—the emotional wounds, unacknowledged fears, and suppressed dreams— acts as barriers not only to our success but to fulfilling our soul's purpose. These barriers keep us tethered to what is familiar, preventing us from tapping into the innate talents and gifts with which we were born to contribute to this journey. It's a subtle confinement, one that can go unnoticed for years, leaving us wondering why, despite our achievements, we feel an inexplicable sense of unfulfillment.

Healing, therefore, is far more than a journey of self-improvement; it is an odyssey of self-discovery and spiritual awakening. By embracing a holistic approach that honors the interconnectedness of mindset, physical sensation, and emotional processing, we embark on a path that leads to deeper levels of healing and fulfillment. This holistic path acknowledges the messages conveyed through our human experiences as crucial insights for our growth, pushing us to confront and heal our unfinished stuff and, in doing so, step out of our boxes.

As we evolve in this process, integrating new pathways for healing, we unlock the possibility of living an extraordinary life—not just one of material success, but one rich with meaning, purpose, and alignment with our soul's deepest desires. This is the essence of true healing: a journey that enables us to transcend the limitations of our human condition and embrace the boundless potential of our spiritual essence.

In committing to this journey, we not only heal ourselves, but also contribute to the collective healing of our world. We shine as beacons of possibility, illustrating that beyond the confines of our safe boxes lies an extraordinary life, waiting to be lived. This is the ultimate fulfillment of our soul's purpose, achieved through the courageous work of facing, feeling, and understanding the profound messages of our human experience.

An Invitation

As our conversation draws to a close, consider this an invitation to a beginning. An invitation to step beyond the familiar shores of mindset-focused development into the vast oceans of holistic integration. This is a call to adventure, to explore the depths of your being and discover the authentic self that lies beneath the surface.

Reflect on the results in each area of your life. Take an honest inventory. What part is calling you to look and begin your transformation? And as you embark on this path, remember, you are not alone. The journey towards wholeness is both personal and universal, a shared human quest for meaning and connection.

If you seek guidance, companionship, or a listening ear as you navigate this journey, know that the invitation to reach out is always open. Together, we can explore the vast landscapes of our being, uncovering the treasures that lie within and forging paths to a more integrated, authentic existence.

The journey to wholeness beckons—will you answer the call?

About Dr. Laurie Emery

Dr. Laurie Emery is more than an author; she's a transformative force for those seeking deep connection and radical change. With a Doctorate in Psychology and over two decades as a transformational coach, she's guided countless individuals towards success in diverse aspects of life.

Her work, through "Build Your Life by Design," revolutionizes the perspectives of entrepreneurs, CEOs, and high achievers, fostering growth, emotional wisdom, and spiritual depth. Dr. Laurie's impact, recognized by accolades like *Business Woman of the Year*, transcends her achievements, touching lives with authenticity and compassion. Her unique blend of psychology, coaching, and spiritual insight doesn't just mark her profession—it's her life's calling.

Dr. Laurie invites us into a journey of self-discovery and profound connection, offering guidance to rewrite our own stories with her as an empowering ally. Engaging with her work isn't merely educational; it's transformative, a step towards personal development in partnership with a visionary leader.

Get Laurie's free gift: www.mind-book.net/gift/Laurie

Defining Moments

By Tracy Carleton, MNLP, MHt, NLP Speaker/Trainer

"Life is a series of defining moments, strung together by passing time. Surrender fully to the moment, because it is not in the moment that defines us, but how we choose to live in it."–Anonymous.

Everyone has a story. And if we'd slow down for just a second to realize this, we'd collectively take one small step for a better mankind. I've heard it said before to BE KIND. Everyone you meet is fighting a battle of some kind or another.

Years ago, I was diagnosed with high-functioning PTSD. I've had an uneducated understanding of post-traumatic stress by thinking that it was caused by exposure to extreme situations or witnessing such acts as our servicemen do during wars. I've learned that this is not the case. To understand the effects of how stress affects the body and mind, I need to go way back. Back to conception.

In my next few paragraphs, I want to clarify that I in no way, shape, or form point fingers at anyone, especially my mother for the circumstances she found herself in 1969 and thereafter. On the contrary. She did her absolute best with little means and, with her unrelenting love, tenacity, and drive, worked hard to raise a couple of exceptional kids.

Many studies have been done to quash what scientists, doctors, and other medical professionals once thought regarding the developing embryo. It was once believed that the forming fetus held no real capacity to experience emotions, among other things. However, recent scientific studies have proven through state-of-the-art experiments and testing that this is not the case. Unborn babies **can feel** and **experience** emotions. When a stressed mother is carrying a baby, the baby is inundated with those stress hormones and, therefore, is born in a stressed state. This state of stress stays with the baby throughout his or her life unless managed. It creates chemical and biological changes that affect the baby. The stressed mother, through conception, or even a stressed caregiver, through spending time with a growing baby during formative months and years, both contribute to the baby's stress levels. These babies are unequipped to regulate them, and this condition causes a lifetime of problems.

The previous was to briefly detail and explain what most babies endure through the simple beauty of childbirth, me included. I believe that new mothers, parents, and family members don't understand the full concept of this life-changing event and its effects on helpless, innocent babies. If we did, we'd pay closer attention to the care we give ourselves and the environments and people we surround ourselves with while carrying them. Many people don't have the luxury or ability or option to change environments, but we all can change our minds. Awareness here is key.

I pause right here to discuss high-functioning PTSD. Post-Traumatic Stress Disorder is described as a mental health condition that's triggered by a terrifying event — either experiencing it or witnessing it. PTSD symptoms can include flashbacks, nightmares, severe anxiety, and uncontrollable thoughts about the event.

From my experiences, and they start young, I have lived a lifetime in fear. I was exposed to extreme situations and witnessed life-changing events, too many to explain here. In recent years, my husband would blame unresolved trauma from things that I experienced for creating a sense of unsteady footing. He'd say I was always, "Waiting for the other shoe to drop." I was jumpy and scared by noise, sound, or sudden movements that I didn't expect. I was on edge a lot. They call it high-functioning for a reason. I have been able to stay busy my whole life. I always find something to occupy my mind. Note: I did not say occupy my time, but my overactive mind.

A few years ago, I sought guidance from a professional to counsel me through the grief of losing my in-laws unexpectedly. With the skill and training that mental health professionals have, my therapist took me *WAY* back to things that had happened in my life that I brushed off, saying, "It's just life." And the funny thing is, I proudly wore a badge of strength to have endured so many unpleasant events. I asked him if I could just mentally dismiss them. I was in harm's way throughout my childhood and teen years and have experienced prolonged stress throughout my entire life. It felt like too much to process. When the subject of forgiveness came up, his answer to my question was, "You can't paint over rust" and it gave me pause to realize there was a lifetime of things to unpack.

I'm reminded of another time in my life in the early 2000s. I was in a tough situation, as many find themselves throughout life. Just as life was heading in a happy and promising direction, the sudden and unexpected full custody of my then-husband's three daughters, ages two to six, took a huge toll on me. They were removed from an unhealthy environment which resulted in behavioral issues that I was not educated, experienced, or otherwise prepared for. I had just turned 25 and welcomed my first child into the world. We bought a house, and I was adamant that I would provide my children with a better upbringing. A stable one with safety and unconditional love. Life was good - until it wasn't.

Because of my faith, I'd pray for strength and there was a call upon my heart to provide help and hope to others who were facing or have faced the same life-altering circumstances I had. For He (God) brought me to it and praise God, He brought me through it. It is said that God allows us to go through suffering and He has a purpose and a plan for it. That was my mission and purpose, so I dove into personal development material from respected individuals, such as Steven Covey and Tony Robbins. I had experienced and made it through so many things that would allow me to relate and be relatable to others having gone or going through similar situations. However, I had to get myself right first before I could offer any empowering, inspiring, and most importantly, practical and sustainable advice and support. It turned out I had a lot more life to live first. That marriage didn't work out in the end. After 17 years of stress and conflict, resulting in an unpleasant environment, I just couldn't stay.

Fast forward several years later, at the height of the pandemic, in 2020, my mom was diagnosed with multiple myeloma. Wow. 2021 was a blur. I received news that a friend of mine was killed in a murder-suicide. A few months later, my mom contracted COVID, and even though all precautions for her health and wellness were in place and she was making positive improvements, and responding well to chemotherapy, my brother and I were met with the painful decision to take her off life support. And a few months later, another friend was celebrating a friend's birthday, and while walking to her car, a speeding fire truck rushing to an accident, hit the building she was walking in front of. She was buried in the rubble.

The restrictions of COVID, the isolation, the grief, and the trauma, all combined with sudden silence, were difficult. I felt the effects of high-functioning PTSD and I was no longer functioning in a way I was proud of. I learned that since I have lived most of my life in survival mode, my already heightened fight-or-flight mechanism was triggered often. Even when there was no real danger. This is called the amygdala hijack. The feeling is unpleasant. It is felt throughout the entire body when triggered. Making one feel the need to defend and protect or get to safety. I was reacting to various things, and it wasn't the "me" everyone, let alone myself, knew. I couldn't bounce back from adversity like I once used to.

Emotions that are not acknowledged or expressed mix and swirl together and can emerge as anger. They pile up and pile up. Feelings were not meant to be suppressed, let alone stay suppressed. In fact, they refuse to. So, what happens is little episodes of irritability that can, and often will, surface. Unfortunately, this can sometimes hurt others.

I put an end to a very slippery slope. I refused to buy into the "victim of circumstance" concept. Although many of the things I had gone through were not my fault, not even close, I knew I had to take responsibility for my thoughts, actions, emotions, and behaviors because of them. After a lot of inner work, it occurred to me I had been running empty my entire life, so I made a promise to myself and to my mom that I would bring awareness to the things that go unnoticed in life since many of us are living our lives on autopilot. Weaving in and out of circumstances and situations. Another bad day. More bad news. More apologies for losing our cool, more regret, and more missed opportunities. My passion is to empower others to make healthy decisions and to react in ways that bring them closer to the life they desire.

I spent hundreds of hours in classroom certification training taught by experienced professionals from the respected company Transform Destiny. They are in the top 1% of international coaches and practitioners and I learned valuable tools and resources to understand my life better.

Why I do things and think the way I do, and to banish negative emotions, eliminate negative beliefs, and get to the root causes of *why*. It has been a liberating and freeing experience. So, I am sharing it with others. My mentor refers to it as the "ripple effect" and I want to be another ripple sharing hope and love with others.

According to the National Institute of Mental Health, statistics show that "Mental illnesses are common in the United States. It is estimated that more than one in five U.S. adults live with a mental illness (57.8 million in 2021). Mental illnesses include many conditions that vary in severity, ranging from mild to moderate to severe." Depression and anxiety are the top two diagnoses that adults, and even children, experience.

Our minds weren't created to feel the sadness, overwhelm, and despair that run rampant amongst most of us. The good news is our brains can protect us from certain experiences until we're ready to process them. This is called our subconscious mind. It stores vast echoes of experience, every memory, it is the domain for all emotions, represses memories with unresolved negative emotions, and will present memories for resolution, among so many other directives. It is so powerful, and it is possible to release the trauma that has been subconsciously repressed. The brain can even be rewired!

There have been so many advances in brain and mind sciences, the conscious and subconscious minds, and neuroscience, all of which contribute to evidence-based personal development and improvement. There are a lot of scientific facts and medical terms that can be confusing, so I will do my best to explain the way I understand and learn.

Neuroplasticity shows that whatever is focused on builds a neural network in the brain. These thoughts become one's identity because they become the words, then actions, and behaviors. Thoughts are powerful and what is focused on grows. If we think and then do the same things every day, all day, for months and years, the neurons fire off in the same paths they are used to. Some call it the superhighway. It's natural. Henry Ford is noted for his inspiring, thought-provoking quotes. He said, "If you always do what you've always done, you'll always get what you always got." I wonder if he knew how profoundly accurate he was.

Let me tell you how easy it is to break habits, have more fulfilling relationships, achieve personal outcomes (goals), and live a simple, more profound, and dynamic life! To go from a dark path to a sidewalk to the superhighway that is available for everyone to cruise on. The habits and thoughts that rule our minds (thus exploding into our behaviors and our identity). DO SOMETHING DIFFERENT! The neurons in our brains are used to the norm and status quo. They flow with familiar frequency and on familiar pathways. Do something different. Think differently. Continued repetitiveness increases the speed of connecting new neural pathways. It may feel uncomfortable at first. A mentor of mine sums it up like this: Pretend you've been wearing one sneaker on a foot and a high heel on the other for many years. After a while, it becomes normal for you as you adjust to your different walking conditions and environments. Imagine taking the high heel off and replacing it with another sneaker. It would feel odd at first. You'd laugh while experiencing little speed bumps along the way. But, while continually wearing two sneakers, it would become like second nature! There's no race or gentle stroll you couldn't face. And last, every negative thought needs to be changed immediately! Come from a place of love before you react. We ALL have this power.

It doesn't stop there! Our brains and minds are the epicenter for all other physiology. And the good news is that we all can learn to improve our lives. However, it is not only what we learn, but what we _unlearn_ that can and will make a difference.

I want you to know that **DEFINING MOMENTS** in life are inevitable. They do **NOT** have to **DEFINE YOU**!

In the end, I have one question for you. From the music group Switchfoot:

This is your life. Are you who you want to be?

About Tracy Carleton, MNLP, MHt, NLP Speaker/Trainer

 As the founder of Transcending Excellence, Tracy Carleton is a highly skilled professional in Neuro-Linguistic Programming (NLP), Hypnotherapy, and Mindfulness. She uses her expertise to assist her clients in eliminating stress, achieving their goals, removing limiting beliefs, and overcoming negative emotions. Through her tailored coaching sessions and workshops, Tracy empowers individuals to create their best lives and reach new heights of success in both their personal and professional endeavors.

Tracy is Board-Certified through the International Board of Coaches and Practitioners and is also an NLP Speaker and Trainer. She connects with diverse audiences and delivers impactful messages.

Tracy's dedication to her clients' well-being and success is clear in the results she helps them achieve. Her ability to provide them with the tools they need to thrive sets her apart as a genuine leader in personal growth and development. Tracy Carleton is a beacon of inspiration and transformation, guiding others toward a life of abundance, fulfillment, and excellence.

Get Tracy's free gift: www.mind-book.net/gift/Tracy

The Power of Positive Self-Talk

By Elizabeth Garvey, CCHT, NLPP, EFTP, TTP, CSLC

Grin and bear it. That was the phrase used whenever my parents wanted to silence me. If anything was wrong, I was told this degrading and conditioning phrase. It seems harmless enough, yet the problem was an environment where I could not consider my own needs. Nor was I allowed to have a voice of my own.

Rewind further still, to a baby in the womb. Feeling the distress of a woman who did not want to be pregnant. Then everything goes dark, and the flame is forever vanquished.

The woman goes to have a total hysterectomy, believing the baby is gone, and everything will be okay once the ability to have more children is removed. Imagine her state of mind to find out she was still pregnant... there had been two lives and only one vanquished.

That is the world I entered. The person who was supposed to love me most showed disdain for my existence. The incredible loss of my twin, coupled with not being wanted, was the catalyst for a life of not being able to love myself.

This environment set me up for decades of abuse from others and, more importantly, from myself. I would speak to myself in ways I would never dream of speaking to another. I was always under stress and worried about what others thought of me. Believing the lies that I wasn't smart enough, pretty enough, and that I was too fat. Lies she spoke over me. When I tried to wear makeup or do anything to improve how I looked, I was called unthinkable names and shamed into hiding. And I believed it all and continued to tell myself the same lies.

It wasn't until decades and two abusive marriages later that I learned to love myself. I learned the power of my thoughts and words, the power of positive self-talk.

So, what is self-talk? How you talk to yourself serves as the cornerstone of your mindset and perception, influencing how you see yourself, others, and the world. Your self-talk encompasses the thoughts and inner monologue flowing through your mind, often on autopilot. These thoughts can take on different forms, each with their unique implications for your well-being and personal development.

Positive self-talk involves nurturing a supportive and uplifting inner dialog. It entails affirming yourself, offering words of encouragement, and focusing on your strengths and accomplishments. Engaging in positive self-talk fosters resilience, self-confidence, and a sense of empowerment.

Self-talk patterns often follow predictable pathways, influenced by internal and external factors, such as experiences, core beliefs, and environmental cues, including past conditioning. It operates automatically, outside of conscious awareness. Recognizing these patterns and identifying common triggers is essential for gaining insight into thought processes and initiating positive change.

Negative self-talk is characterized by critical, self-defeating, and pessimistic thoughts. It involves berating yourself for perceived failures, dwelling on shortcomings, and magnifying fears and insecurities. Negative self-talk erodes your self-esteem, fuels self-doubt, and perpetuates cycles of stress and anxiety. It involves cognitive distortions—irrational or exaggerated ways of thinking that distort reality. Common cognitive distortions include black-and-white thinking, catastrophizing, and personalization.

Neutral self-talk falls somewhere in between. It may involve mundane observations, factual statements, or neutral assessments of situations. While not inherently harmful, neutral self-talk may become problematic if it reinforces negative beliefs.

External influences also shape self-talk. Factors like social comparisons, media messages, and interpersonal interactions can trigger self-critical thoughts and reinforce negative beliefs.

By gaining a deeper understanding of the nuances of self-talk, you cultivate greater awareness of your internal dialog, challenge unhelpful patterns, and intentionally cultivate a more positive and empowering mindset. As you explore practical strategies and techniques for harnessing the power of positive self-talk, let's consider how your self-talk influences your emotional well-being, attitudes, and actions.

Positive self-talk isn't just a feel-good concept—it's rooted in neuroscience and psychology.

The Science Behind Positive Self-Talk

As you delve into the neurological and psychological mechanisms that underpin the efficacy of positive self-talk, you'll discover how you can reshape your brain and influence your mental and emotional well-being. Your brain's remarkable ability to reorganize itself in response to new experiences and learning is known as neuroplasticity.

Positive self-talk can reshape neural pathways, rewiring your brain for optimism, resilience, and self-efficacy. Through repeated practice, affirming thoughts and auto-suggestions can strengthen positive neural connections while weakening negative ones.

When you engage in positive self-talk, your mirror neurons may simulate the experience of receiving encouragement and support from others, further reinforcing your sense of self-worth and confidence. Mirror neurons are specialized brain cells that fire when you act *and* when you observe someone else acting. These neurons play a crucial role in empathy, social learning, and imitation.

Positive self-talk can also stimulate the release of neurotransmitters such as dopamine, serotonin, and endorphins—chemical messengers associated with feelings of pleasure, happiness, and well-being. By boosting levels of these neurotransmitters, positive self-talk can enhance your mood, reduce stress, and promote emotional resilience.

Conversely, negative self-talk triggers your brain's stress response, flooding your body with cortisol and other stress hormones. Chronic stress can have detrimental effects on physical and mental health, contributing to inflammation, impaired immune function, and mood and sleep disorders. In contrast, positive self-talk can dampen the stress response, promoting relaxation, and restoring physiological balance.

Positive self-talk has been shown to enhance performance in various domains, including sports, academics, and professional endeavors. Athletes who use positive self-talk techniques report greater confidence, focus, and resilience in the face of competition.

It is associated with improved health outcomes, including faster recovery from illness and surgery, reduced pain perception, and enhanced immune function. Optimistic individuals engage in healthier behaviors, such as regular exercise, nutritious eating, and seeking medical care when needed.

By understanding the neurobiological and psychological mechanisms underlying positive self-talk, you can appreciate its profound impact on your mental, emotional, and physical well-being. Armed with this knowledge, you can harness the power of positive self-talk to cultivate a resilient mindset and unlock your full potential for growth and fulfillment.

Tools to Encourage Positive Self-Talk

Keeping a **journal** can serve as a valuable tool for identifying negative self-talk patterns. Take the time to write thoughts and emotions in response to challenging situations or triggers. By examining the journal entries, you can uncover recurring patterns, common cognitive distortions, and the impact of negative self-talk on your mood and behavior.

Specific events, situations, or interactions can trigger negative self-talk by activating underlying insecurities or fears. Reflect on the circumstances that elicit negative thoughts and emotions. Are there recurring themes or triggers that provoke self-critical or pessimistic responses? By understanding the underlying causes of your negative self-talk, you can begin to **challenge and reframe** these unhelpful thoughts, paving the way for a powerful internal dialog.

When negative self-talk arises, you can engage in **cognitive restructuring** by questioning the validity of your thoughts. Asking whether the thought is based on fact or interpretation. Challenging it by examining the evidence that supports or contradicts the belief. Consider how you would respond to a friend in a similar situation, offering yourself the same kindness and understanding.

Evaluate the validity of your negative self-talk through **reality testing**. Gathering objective evidence and considering alternative perspectives to challenge catastrophic thinking. Reflect on the likelihood and severity of potential outcomes. And practice self-compassion by extending kindness to yourself, especially during moments of self-doubt or adversity.

Counteract negative self-talk with **affirmations** that reinforce your worth, capabilities, and potential. Creating a list of affirmations aligned with your values and goals and repeating them. Focus on affirmations that are realistic, specific, and uplifting, using them as a powerful tool to combat self-doubt and cultivate self-confidence.

Also, cultivate **mindfulness** to observe negative thoughts without judgment or attachment. When negative self-talk arises, gently redirect attention to the present moment. Engaging in mindfulness meditation to deepen awareness of thoughts, emotions, and body sensations, fostering inner peace and resilience.

By implementing these techniques, you can challenge negative self-talk patterns, break free from self-limiting beliefs, and cultivate a more compassionate and empowering inner dialog. This journey of self-discovery and personal growth holds the potential to transform your relationship with yourself and enhance your overall well-being.

Transforming Past Conditioning

The most recent change I made was to disarm the command to grin and bear it once and for all. This command had caused a lot of grief and misunderstanding in my life. My brother had shattered his elbow in a fall. He had surgery and had pins sticking out of the elbow. He asked me to help him clean and bandage the wound. Every time he winced in pain, I giggled. Not because I thought it was funny or because I enjoyed hurting him. That nervous giggle and goofy smile was a programmed response. I was literally grinning while bearing a stressful situation.

Realizing this command was why I acted that way came much later, years later. I was in a counseling session with my oldest son. He brought up a mutual trauma memory that I was uncomfortable talking about, so I unconsciously grinned while shaking my head no. I didn't even realize I had grinned until my son had a meltdown. He thought I was laughing at his pain, our pain.

That entire weekend, I meditated on why my son thought I would ever laugh at our trauma. That was when I realized I was still acting on the command to grin and bear it, decades after it had been given. When I realized it was old programming still unconsciously operating in my life, I used my tools as a hypnotherapist to remove this program. I removed the command from my timeline; past, present, and future. Since then, I have been aware of times I would have grinned before and now I allow my face to express my genuine emotions as I feel them.

This has been a journey of self-discovery and learning how to speak to myself with kindness and love. I could have beaten myself up for the program I was still running. Instead, I had grace for myself, and I apologized to my son. I told him about the programming and the phrase I had been conditioned with, and that I was sorry for how it affected him.

That one act of changing how I behaved unconsciously, and being gentle with myself, coupled with apologizing to him, has changed the dynamic between my son and me. He understands that, like him, I also suffered from trauma and abuse in my childhood and am still walking out of that pain. I showed compassion for myself and him in my moment of awareness.

Celebrate Every Step

As you move forward from this chapter, carry forward the valuable wisdom and insights gained. Commit to cultivate a kinder, more supportive relationship with yourself, grounded in self-compassion, self-acceptance, and self-love. Through mastering your internal dialog, you open doors to infinite possibilities, empowering you to shape the life you deeply desire.

Keep in mind that the path toward positive self-talk may not always be straightforward, and setbacks are a natural part of the journey. Celebrate every step of progress and never underestimate the profound impact of your thoughts. With dedication, persistence, and a belief in your potential, you hold the power to rewrite the narrative of your life and step into a future brimming with promise and purpose.

About Elizabeth Garvey, CCHT, NLPP, EFTP, TTP, CSLC

Elizabeth Garvey is a Clinical Hypnotherapist and Sleep Coach at usleepnow.com. She is IBCP board certified in Hypnotherapy, NLP, EFT, TIME Techniques, and Life Coaching.

Elizabeth loves to help veterans, first responders, and their families because her dad was a Vietnam Veteran. She watched him struggle with insomnia and PTSD after service and saw its effects on him and the whole family.

Elizabeth advocates for sleep as the cornerstone of well-being, crafting tailored plans to assist clients in reclaiming tranquility and pursuing a fulfilling life.

Recognized as an engaging speaker, Elizabeth shares her expertise on subjects such as mental health, emotional intelligence, and sleep through enlightening talks at conferences, workshops, and podcasts.

Elizabeth is also co-author and editor of the best-selling books "Becoming Positively Awesome: Transform Your Life Through the Power of Positive Thinking," and "All the Answers Are Within: Learning to Trust Your Inner Guidance."

To learn more about her work, visit https://www.linkedin.com/in/coachgarvey

Get Elizabeth's gift: www.mind-book.net/gift/Elizabeth

Create Your Life on Purpose

By Joanne Klepal–Master of Change & Transformation

Do you wake up dreading the idea of spending another day at an unfulfilling job? Do you feel that most days you're on autopilot? Maybe you feel stuck; in life, in a relationship, doing the things that you were "supposed" to do, and now question "why" or question "what's the purpose?" Perhaps you just feel the need to be a part of something bigger and more meaningful.

Who are you, here in this body, this lifetime? Are you here to play the game or watch the game? Are you the "star" of your movie or just the "extra?"

If you know there is more to life than what you've been experiencing, then it is time to wake up.

Fifteen years ago, I found myself so stuck I felt paralyzed and didn't know what to do, where to go, what I wanted, or how to go about it. I had run into a dead-end.

I had an epiphany that I had been in a toxic marriage that had all the same patterns I had grown up with as a child, particularly around various types of abuse and alcoholism.

It was impossible to conceive that I could "create" my life, let alone live my life on purpose; instead, I was just fumbling along.

I came to a point where I felt I had had enough and didn't want to live the rest of my life as I had been- dying, not living.

147

Once I began mastering my mindset and started creating my life on purpose, many doors opened.

I partnered with a Neuro-Linguistic Programming (NLP) trained transformation coach in what he called a "breakthrough" session. The only way I could describe it was a complete mental, emotional, and energetic detox.

Although I did not understand the process then, I knew something had shifted as I began seeing life through a new lens and began doing things I could never conceive of, like traveling the world solo, publishing books, and changing careers.

This was a pivotal point in my life. It saved me in so many ways, mentally, physically, emotionally, and put my life on a new trajectory; it was like a complete reset and the beginning to the rest of my life.

Back then, I had zero self-awareness. I was unsure of what to expect or how potent the breakthrough experience would be. The sheer creativity behind the process was awe-inspiring. I'll do my best to share some key highlights for you here.

How a Personal Breakthrough Experience Works

Imagine you have a blank canvas in your yard to create a garden from scratch. You plant seeds, trees, flowers, vegetables, fruits, and watch as they grow and blossom into vibrant colors, you enjoy their luscious floral scents and savor their delicious tastes. Then, you get busy; you stop paying attention; you stop tending your garden, and over time, as it's ignored, it becomes overgrown, full of weeds, disease, rotten fruits, and the once vibrant plants die. The garden is now so overgrown, suffocating and stagnating under the weeds, disease, and invasive plants that have taken over, that there is just no room to plant anything healthy and new.

Like your mind, at birth, you start with a blank canvas. Seeds are then planted throughout your life by others (parents, teachers, society) and their experiences, and by you and your experiences. These seeds are your values, beliefs, thoughts, and emotions.

With time, your autopilot switches on and you stop tending your mind. You don't pull the old weeds from their roots or clear the decay or diseased plants, and therefore you don't have room for new, healthy growth. You stagnate and are invaded with negative mindsets, negative thoughts, negative emotions, and limiting decisions and beliefs. Then you suffocate so much in this stagnation that it leaves you stuck, making poor decisions, repeating old patterns, and behaviors, and being frustrated with your life.

You have a choice to continue as you are, or change; and it's never too late to change you, to change your life.

A breakthrough experience clears the debris of your old limiting beliefs, thoughts, emotions, and patterns that are deeply rooted in your subconscious and brings them to light, to your conscious awareness, resulting in positive learnings, empowering beliefs and empowered thoughts, and a complete mind shift. Now, you can master your mind. Now, you have made space to create a new, healthy garden, to create your life and your future on purpose.

What's Important

Have you ever taken the time to think about what's important to you in your relationships, career, family, health, wealth, etc.? Many of you take off running in life without a clear direction, doing things you're told you're "supposed" to do (go to university, get a job, get married, have kids), but you're not taught to think about what it is YOU want before sprinting off, so you fumble and fall until you run into a dead-end.

During my first personal breakthrough experience, I was asked profound questions which made me consider aspects of my life in unique ways.

I was asked to **take stock** of where I was in various parts of my life, such as family, career, finance, spiritual, relationships, personal development, and so on. I then reflected on where I wanted to be, and the gap helped home in on the focus of my breakthrough session.

For my focus area, I then identified my *values* and what was most important to me, like what's most important to me about my career. Until then, I never realized how fundamental values are. Values are like the spark and fire that drives everything I do and don't do in life. For example, if I don't value working out to get fit, I'm just not going to do it, no matter how beneficial I "know" it may be. I can buy that gym membership and go a few times, but I guarantee you, it won't last.

These questions may seem simplistic, but they are the type of questions I had never been asked in my 40 years of life, and until then, never pondered. This was a fundamental and powerful starting point.

Clear the Debris

Dead plants, diseased leaves, rotten fruit, and vegetables — these are all symptoms of a bigger problem. Picking the rotten fruit or plucking the diseased leaves may make the garden look good on the surface but doesn't resolve the underlying cause. To do this, you must dig deeper to get to the root cause of the problems you are experiencing.

Have you done something you know you "shouldn't do", or not done something you know you "should do", but continue repeating those old patterns instead? Have you continuously been in unhealthy relationships, eaten unhealthily, sabotaged career opportunities, and so on?

These are just symptoms of deeper seeded, unconscious root causes from outdated belief systems, outdated values, outdated experiences. Maybe you didn't receive the approval from a parent growing up. Maybe it was drilled into you not to speak to strangers, or you were told "children are to be seen and not heard", and now as an adult you're afraid to speak up, are petrified of speaking in public, or you'd prefer to hide in the corner of a room and not be seen.

To clear the debris, in a personal breakthrough experience, you must first understand the problem and how you do the problem to get to the root cause. Based on this, your breakthrough coach can determine which tools will best assist you in clearing out the old debris.

There are too many tools to mention in this chapter, so here are a couple that had a significant impact on my experience:

As mentioned, simple, yet **powerful questions** can help to understand the problem, reframe the problem, and push beyond the boundaries of the problem.

When you have a problem, you only see "the problem" and not the infinite solutions available. It's like being the cereal in a cereal box; you're confined and only see the cereal within the box, and not what's outside the box.

For example: *"How is that a problem?"*, *"What's the purpose of the problem?"*, *"How is the problem serving you?"*, *"How do you know you have the problem?"*, and *"How do you do the problem?"*

During my first breakthrough, I felt frustrated and confused by many of the questions. This was because I was thinking from the conscious thought, whereas the questions work with your deep subconscious mind, where true, lasting change takes place. I had to put my logic aside and remind myself to just *"trust the process"*. Once the problem is understood, the clearing can begin.

Have you hung on to old emotions, feeling anger, sadness, hurt, guilt for events that happened in childhood? Maybe you were jilted and haven't let go.

It's been proven that holding on to negative emotions (root cause) has a direct impact on your health (symptoms). For instance, if you hold on to inappropriate anger, you may experience heart problems.

T.I.M.E™ Techniques is a tool which helps get to the root cause of any inappropriate negative emotions, limiting decisions, and limiting beliefs. You can then see past events, decisions, and beliefs, from a more neutral perspective, allowing you to discover new learnings. This is a powerful and liberating process.

I'm sure you've heard the saying, "not forgiving someone is like drinking poison expecting the other person to die." Another powerful tool used in clearing the debris is an ancient Hawaiian practice of **forgiveness** called Ho'oponopono and can be interpreted to "make right twice."

In this practice, you can choose to forgive yourself and others (knowing that we all do the best we can with what we have). It enables you to cut the energetic cord, which ties you to another person, freeing you both.

Making changes within yourself transforms the world around you.

Create Your Future

Once the debris is cleared and the root causes are resolved, you have a solid foundation to create your life with a clean slate and a fresh new, empowered mindset, which enables you to create the life you want and deserve.

In creating your future, creating your life on purpose, you must first know what you want, to know where to begin.

Another powerful exercise my coach took me through was to review my values again from scratch. My values at the end of this process were profoundly different and much more positive compared to the ones previously identified at the start of the breakthrough session.

When I began the process, I knew what I didn't want in my life, but I struggled with identifying what I truly wanted. My coach posed two deep, thought provoking, and life-changing questions which I go back to time and time again. *"What would you do if you knew you couldn't fail?"* and *"What is your purpose?"*

From here, I created a particular goal and programmed this into the future using T.I.M.E™ Techniques mentioned. I let it go and then followed two key elements for creating lasting change, including:

- *Taking action*, which may include changing behaviors, changing situations and circumstances, establishing or reinforcing new boundaries. Nothing happens if you don't act, right?

- *Focusing on what you want*, not what you don't want. You've heard the saying where your focus goes, energy flows.

In my first breakthrough session, I discovered a major root cause of many of my symptoms was a lack of self-love. I felt unworthy and believed I was unlovable. Releasing these disempowered beliefs and emotions took a significant weight off my shoulders. It allowed me to embrace and accept myself, my voice, my being, just as I am. I felt I was rediscovering myself again.

The result was the start of the rest of my life. The start of creating my life on purpose, with purpose and being the "star", not an "extra."

Now, my greatest joy is being able to help you transform, as I was, through this powerful breakthrough experience.

There is nothing else in this world more satisfying than seeing you transform. Witnessing you to release the debris that has held you back for so long. Seeing you soar beyond your wildest imaginations. Watching you live your dreams and your life on purpose!

About Joanne Klepal- Master of Change & Transformation

 Joanne Klepal is the founder of Live Your Yellow Brick Road and YogaMeetsU.com. She is a master of change and transformation, with an intense passion for continuous personal growth and development.

Joanne's purpose is to empower women to get unstuck, enabling them to create and live their life on purpose, with purpose.

She brings a unique experience to personal transformation by leveraging both the "science" of change; Neurolinguistics, Hypnosis, and Coaching, with the "art" of change; her skills in Mindfulness and Energy practices.

She is a Certified Master Practitioner of Neuro-Linguistic Programming & NLP Coaching, Certified Master Practitioner of T.I.M.E. ™ Techniques, Certified Clinical Hypnotherapist, Certified Change Management Professional™, Certified Reiki Master Trainer, Kundalini Yoga Teacher, a breathwork practitioner, and author of *Natural Healing Techniques, Get Well & Stay Well with Asian Bio-Energetic Therapy.*

To find out more about Joanne and Personal Breakthrough Experience visit: www.liveyouryellowbrickroad.com

Get Joanne's free gift: www.mind-book.net/gift/Joanne

From Terrible Two's to Terrific Toddlers
Empowering Your Family to Embrace a Growth Mindset

By Dr. Christine Anderson, DC, DICCP, FABCDD, DiHom

Toddler's strong-willed behavior comes from their innate desire for independence and sense of control, not deliberate defiance. Parents can create a harmonious environment by remaining calm, setting healthy boundaries, and having strategies in place. Embracing a growth mindset empowers the entire family to thrive.

CONDITIONED RESPONSE AND TANTRUMS

Remember Pavlov's experiments with dogs and the concept of the "conditioned response" from your science classes? By pairing the bell with giving meat, an association was created where the bell alone triggered salivation–a "conditioned response" that wouldn't normally occur on its own.

In this same way, how you respond to your child's tantrums can shape their behavior and create a "conditioned response." The more attention given to your child during tantrums, the more likely they will become a coping mechanism for your child and a way to get your attention.

Understanding WHY toddlers have tantrums is crucial for prevention. Limited language skills often lead to frustration when they can't express their wants and needs. Teaching basic words, like yes, no, more, food, and tired can help.

Anticipating and fulfilling your child's needs is key to preventing meltdowns caused by hunger, thirst, or fatigue. Do not leave home without healthy snacks and water. It is best to leave social situations when you see your child is getting tired. An early bedtime is crucial, so they get the sleep they need and won't be grumpy the next day.

Another common trigger for tantrums is transitioning or ending an activity. When asked to stop an activity they are engaged in abruptly, your child feels powerless and expresses this by crying and resists moving onto the next activity. Set expectations when beginning the activity. Have them help you set a timer or pick a favorite song to play. When the timer goes off or a song finishes, have them help you clean up. Sing a song while you do it or set the timer again for a minute and see if you both can beat the clock.

In my experience, I've found the use of electronics - phones, tablets, computers, and electronic games - or more aptly, stopping their use, is often a tantrum trigger. My advice is to avoid introducing them to babies and young children to prevent potential issues. Because of the effects on their developing brains, electronics should not be used by children under 3 years of age. Of particular concern are cell phones and iPads, as these devices are typically held close to their bodies. Children's smaller size and thinner skull bones make them more susceptible to the effects of Electromagnetic Fields (EMFs). Watch movies with your older toddler on a big screen together, preferably in 20-minute increments, and then discuss it afterwards.

Tantrums can often arise from your child seeking your attention. Ensure you're actively engaging with them in activities they enjoy and exploring new things together. Make it a priority to switch off your phone and give them your undivided attention.

Despite your attempts to head off tantrums, they will occur until your child realizes they won't get attention. Here are some solutions for when tantrums occur that have worked for me with my children and the kids I see in my practice.

- Stay calm to prevent escalation of the situation. Breathe love into your heart and exhale love out to your child. Remember, this behavior is a normal part of development, and what you do next will decide whether it continues.
- Acknowledge your child's "big feelings" without trying to reason with them. They are operating from the emotional part of the brain, which is not receptive to logic.
- Let them know you'll be close by while they express their feelings. Stay within sight, but avoid direct eye contact.
- Engage in an activity that you know they enjoy or play music and dance. As they calm down, talk to yourself about the fun you are having. Your positive energy will encourage them to join you. Distraction and movement can also help to head off meltdowns.
- After they have calmed down, you can use their favorite toy to "ask" why they were crying. This could lead to a discussion about their feelings.

- With your older toddler, this can also lead to a discussion about what they can do when they are having big feelings. Have them come up with potential solutions.

If a toddler is biting, hitting, or throwing things, remove them from the situation promptly. Often, they react out of frustration. Calmly tell them to "be gentle" while gently stroking their arm. "We are nice to our friends/brother/sister/toys. If you want to play with 'X,' then please be nice and gentle." Focus on modeling the desired behavior and tell them the behavior you want to see or hear. Don't say, "Stop hitting!" All they hear is "hit" and no other options for what you would like them to do.

Most importantly, when you see your toddler exhibiting desired behavior, praise their efforts. Say, "I see you are being gentle with 'X.' It feels good to be kind to our friends." Acknowledge positive actions, like asking for food nicely or waiting their turn patiently. "I noticed you could wait your turn without getting upset." You want to link their desired behaviors with your positive attention.

CHOICES WITHIN BOUNDARIES

Kids need boundaries for so many reasons. They need to know that someone else is in charge, so they can relax. They need to know that they are safe and loved for who they are. Boundaries, when enforced, create predictability and a sense of security; they will know what is expected of them and what behaviors are acceptable. This allows them to be more confident in exploring and gaining their independence.

Within those boundaries, you can, and should, give children choices. If you give toddlers the illusion of choice, then they will feel like they have control and they are less apt to rebel and more apt to cooperate.

Goal: Get your toddler dressed! Say, "Do you want to wear the pink dress or the blue one?" What if they want to wear the green one? Great! "Put the green one on and then we will have breakfast. Let me know if you need any help." Wait. Green wasn't a choice. Remember the goal? Get your toddler dressed. If the goal is met, then move on. We are trying to avert power struggles and get the job done with cooperation.

Goal: Eat breakfast! "Do you want a smoothie or cereal?" Notice, I didn't ask, "Do you want breakfast?" This question leaves room for the dreaded "No." I also didn't ask, "What do you want for breakfast?" This question gives too many choices. And notice how I set up breakfast was next after getting dressed in the previous goal? Kids <u>love</u> predictability and routines. Use this to your advantage by "playing dumb" and asking what comes next.

Goal: Having your child eat (preferably green) veggies! "Do you want broccoli or salad for dinner?" "I want carrots!" "Great, you can have carrots, but they need a friend that is green. Do you want broccoli or salad?" Now you've got your child to agree to eat two different colored veggies! If you don't have carrots, then tell your child that they can help you shop for them and maybe you can pick a new veggie to try, too.

I am sure you have the idea by now of what I am saying. Pick the goal you want to achieve, and within that goal, give your child appropriate choices so they feel more in control.

SOME CAVEATS

Do not end your statement with, "Okay?" As in, "It is time for you to go to bed, OK?" "OK," leaves the possibility of your child saying "No! It is not OK!" Set yourself up for success with, "How do you want to go to your bed? Piggyback ride or Airplane?"

Be consistent with the boundaries you have set up. If you are too fluid with them, then your child will not know when they have breached the boundary and out goes that concept of predictability and security. It also will cause some children to keep testing and pushing the boundaries, which can lead to "misbehavior." My older son was this way. I learned early on that if I let him go a millimeter over the boundary, then off he would go. I had to be super strict with him.

If there are consequences for breaching the boundaries, then be consistent about enforcing those consequences. Once your child realizes you don't mean what you say, then you are most likely going to have issues with their behavior. And from my experience, this shows up as bigger behavior issues in school and in the home as they get older. This means that you should not pronounce idle threats you are not prepared to act on. If you don't mean it, don't say it! And yes, consequences could elicit a tantrum, but we already covered that. Over time, when your child trusts you will follow through with consequences, then there will be less probability that they will act up.

The consequences should match the behavior and age of your child. As simply as possible, tell your child, in advance, of what you expect of them and the consequences that will occur if those expectations are not met. Make sure they understand by getting a nod or a "yes." They have now agreed to this behavior "contract," so to speak. "Be gentle with your friends. If you don't play nicely with your friends, then we will go home and that would be sad." Get a "yes" they understand. If they are less than gentle with their friends, then you would say, "I am sorry you hit your friend. Now we will have to go home. I am sure next time you will make a better choice and be gentle with your friend."

EMPOWERING A GROWTH MINDSET

Let's discuss the importance of a growth mindset for both your child and the entire family. According to psychologist and researcher Carol S. Dweck, PhD, a growth mindset cultivates self-motivation and a love of learning. Failures and mistakes are considered opportunities to learn and grow. Obstacles are met with determination, since those with a growth mindset believe they have the power to change their circumstances through effort.

People with a fixed mindset believe abilities like intelligence or talent are innate - you either have them, or you don't. If something is too hard, then you cannot be "smart" and, therefore, you are "dumb." If other players, artists, and musicians are "more talented" than you, then you "stink at football, art, flute, etc." Those with a fixed mindset give up without trying when faced with obstacles; "trying" offers an opportunity to fail, and failing is synonymous with "being a failure." With a fixed mindset, you are a victim to your circumstances; someone or something else is always to blame.

We've all used both mindsets at different times, but one strategy typically dominates. Do you know which mindset you gravitate towards? If it's a growth mindset, fantastic! If it is a fixed mindset, great! Not the response you expected, I bet. Once you acknowledge you have a fixed mindset, then you can actively shift your beliefs to cultivate more growth mindset attributes. When you model a growth mindset, then your child will mirror your responses to challenges and "mistakes." Therefore, mindset matters for the whole family.

Here are some tips for empowering a growth mindset:

- Start early. Even babies are subconsciously soaking up what you are doing, saying, and feeling.
- Model a growth mindset in your daily activities. Verbalize your process of overcoming obstacles and mistakes.
- Let them see how you handle an "OOPS" moment. "OOPS" being an "Outstanding Opportunity Presenting Itself Suddenly." This will help them learn to be more resilient.
- Use positive language during a challenge such as, "I can't do it yet, but I know it will get easier the more I keep trying and learning."

- Praise your child's efforts and learning process, especially when trying and learning new things.
- DO NOT praise their intelligence, talent, looks, or abilities.
- Don't help them unless they ask for help. And even when you help them, assist as little as possible.
- Celebrate "failures," and "mistakes."
- Celebrate their progress in an endeavor and the results of their efforts when they complete a task.
- Encourage curiosity to foster a lifelong love of learning.
- Try new things together as a family.

I love toddlers–they are so much fun! My growth mindset has served me well not only in raising my three children, but also in working with toddlers in my office. Toddlers are one of the trickiest age groups to adjust, but I use their natural love of play and imagination to garner their cooperation. It is always worth investing a little extra time to make sure they feel safe and heard, and have some control over what is going on.

Now that you have a better understanding of why toddlers have tantrums and some tools for preventing and handling them, you can be empowered to change your situation and enjoy the toddler years. Parenting is difficult, but it is worth the reward when you see your children grow up resilient with a love of learning and lust for life.

If the growth mindset part of you is hungry for more, follow me on social media for more ways to help your kids and family grow up happy and healthy in mind-body-spirit.

About Dr. Christine Anderson, DC, DICCP, FABCDD, DiHom

 Dr. Christine Anderson is a Pediatric Chiropractor with over 33 years of experience. She graduated Summa Cum Laude from CCC-LA with a Doctorate in Chiropractic, a post graduate Board Certification in Chiropractic Pediatrics & Pregnancy (DICCP), Certification in Functional Neurology and Childhood Developmental Disorders (FABCDD) and a Diploma in Homeopathy (DiHom). Dr. Anderson is committed to enhancing the body and brain function of babies, children, pregnant women, and those with special needs globally.

Dr. Anderson has taught for the Chiropractic Pediatrics & Pregnancy Program and has been a featured speaker at the ICA Pediatrics' yearly conferences. As a mother of three children, "Dr. Chris" brings a unique perspective to her practice with understanding the challenges and joys of raising a family.

Dr. Chris' passion for helping people release physical, emotional, and toxic stress in their lives shines through in her work at the Kid Chiropractic Family Wellness Center in Los Angeles, as well as throughout the world with online support. Go to www.LosAngeles-Chiropractor.com to learn more now!

Get Christine's free gift: www.mind-book.net/gift/Christine

Mastery of the Mind

The Power of Letting Go

By Ronald Lance, NLPMP, MTT, MHt, MSC

Today, the breakup of a relationship or a divorce is all too common. Most of us have been through this in our lives.

When I started my divorce business intending to help people. I saw way too many couples get dragged through the process for years. Seeing this, I made the process as quick and painless as I could.

Making the process fast and affordable, I felt satisfied I was helping my clients. However, I noticed many were suffering from grief after the divorce process was over. They had a difficult time letting go of the past and the hurt.

I found people feel that they will never be the same, will never date, or get married again. These are all very natural responses. I have heard them thousands of times.

People try to deal with what they feel is the shattered pieces of their lives and try to get pieces of their lives back together. The problem is not the divorce but the grief that is left after the breakup or divorce.

Once they deal with the grief, questions come up such as:

"What did I do wrong?"

"What could I have done to prevent this from happening?"

"Why did they leave me?"

These are all too common.

Whatever the reason for the breakup, the lingering emotional connection and grief can make it difficult to move on with life, and therein lies the problem.

Most people try to deal with the emotions on their own without seeking help from anyone. Family and friends try to be supportive and tell them that everything will be ok. However, without help, it takes a long time until you are ok.

People linger with these emotions, and it can take years to recover from the grief.

The problem for most people is that they cannot let go, so they relive the relationship over and over in their minds. They repeatedly tell their family and friends their story.

"That's where we first met."

"That's where we went on our first date."

"We loved going there."

"That was our favorite restaurant."

Then the questions start all over.

"Why did they do this to me?"

Or worse yet, they hold it inside and don't allow anyone in. They keep reliving the past over and over in their mind and thus have trouble letting go of the relationship and moving forward.

Some people are held in grief until they experience depression. I have even seen people get to the point of being prescribed anti-depressants.

And the media doesn't help. While they are dealing with the grief, they notice every single break up song on the radio.

Song like:

Why Does It Hurt So Bad by Whitney Houston

When I was Your Man by Bruno Mars

What Hurts the Most by Rascal Flatts

What's Left of Me by Nick Lachey

Torn by Natalia Imbruglia

Un-Break My Heart by Tony Braxton

Ain't No Sunshine by Bill Withers

This is just a few of the thousands of songs out there reminding sufferers of the struggle with grief, taking them further into sadness.

After listening to all those songs, then there are the quotes dealing with grief.

Quotes such as:

"Sometimes, your worst enemy, is your memory. Let it go."
-Anonymous.

"Tears are the silent language of grief."
-Voltaire.

"Good memories are the ones that hurt the most."
-Anonymous.

After all this, you can clearly see the problem.

I tell my clients that grief does not kill you, BUT it prevents you from living and moving on. Since so many of my clients were struggling. I started searching for a solution to help them.

And I found a solution. What I discovered is that hypnosis solves the problem of grief. So, I started learning everything I could, taking classes, and mastering many techniques. I became a Master Hypnotherapist.

Now, many of my divorce clients schedule hypnosis sessions to deal with the grief after their divorce. The hypnosis session minimizes the grief emotions that are holding them back.

This is great for clients that live in my area, but I started thinking about other people in need. I started searching for a solution to that problem as well. I discovered the there are two hypnosis options that can be used anywhere.

The first option is to seek a local hypnotherapist. Look for a certified hypnotherapist in your area that can help you to let go of grief and move on. They will not remove the memories. What they will do is release the grief associated with the memories.

A hypnotherapist will put you into a state of deep relaxation and reduce the emotion associated with grief. You will be so relaxed that you will enjoy it. Find a hypnotist on the internet close to where you live, then call and schedule an appointment. They will explain the entire process and answer questions that you may have. After the session, you will see the problem of grief in a different light.

I also discovered that many closed their office because of COVID-19 and started seeing clients over zoom. This gives you access to hypnotherapists around the world.

The second option is to use recorded hypnosis. This is a little different from the first. With this option, you will go on the internet to locate a certified hypnotherapist that is selling their downloadable hypnosis session for the release of grief. Once downloaded, find a comfortable place, and just listen to the recording. Most people listen to these from the comfort of their home. Just lay back and listen, that's all you have to do.

Either option will give you the results that you are seeking.

In my practice, I have discovered that hypnosis can take a situation like grief and reduce recovery to as little as one session.

I have been helping so many of my clients for years to move on after their divorce and live happier, wonderful lives.

Hypnosis can assist you with minimizing the emotions that are holding you back, too. Hypnosis will allow you to let go of the past, grief, and negative emotions so that the pain, anxiety, and sadness can be minimized. It will give you the freedom to move forward in your life.

After hypnosis you will find that you have control of your life back, freedom to move on, and create the future that you desire and deserve.

I tell my clients it's time to build the future that you see yourself living in. Starting today, *your future self awaits you*.

This is a new chapter in your life. Embrace it and move on to the life that you deserve.

Create the future you would love to live in.

Let go of the past. The time is now to do all the things that you were prevented from doing in that relationship.

Now is the time to:

Spend time with family.

Go on the vacation you always wanted.

Move to that city you wanted to live in.

Get that education that you wanted.

You see, grief will stop you from living your true potential. However, once you let it go and move on, then your future will become brighter and limitless.

Dream BIG and take action to turn it from a dream into reality.

The only thing holding you back is ACTION.

This is THE POWER OF LETTING GO.

About Ronald Lance, NLPMP, MTT, MHt, MSC

 Ronald Lance is a retired United States Marine Corps Veteran who discovered hypnotherapy. Wanting to learn more, he studied and graduated from Transform Destiny.

Ronald has honed his skills and expertise in guiding individuals towards positive change and personal empowerment. His unwavering commitment to his clients' well-being and success sets him apart as a trusted and respected professional Master Hypnotherapist.

Ronald has years of dedicated service in helping single and divorced individuals. He brings a unique blend of discipline, integrity, and compassion to his practice.

Ronald has solidified his reputation as a leading expert in the industry. He connects with clients on a deep level to help them overcome challenges, heal from past traumas, and achieve their goals for a brighter future.

Go to ChangeYourDestinyNOW.com for more information.

Get Ronald's free gift: www.mind-book.net/gift/Ronald

Transforming Fear into Freedom

By Courtney Gale CCHt, NLPP, PTT, CSC

On a cold day right after my birthday, I got in my car and traveled about two hours and one hundred miles away. I was traveling to pursue something I had always wanted to try... skydiving!

I was so excited that I could not sleep the night before. As I traveled, I wondered, "What will it be like?" "What would I be thinking?" and "How would it feel?" Arriving at the airfield, the magnitude of the endeavor suddenly set in.

I pulled up to a small airfield hidden off a dirt road between two farms. The building was bright yellow with blue trim around the windows. It was cold, and the wind was gusting over the open fields. While parking the car, I noticed out of the corner of my eye the small plane parked off to the side.

I walked in the front door, which looked like a converted house attached to a barn. On the inside, it resembled a cozy living room, and in the corner was a television connected to a VCR with a tape of previous sky dives being played. Now, I was stoked.

I was alone in the office. I looked at the photos on the wall, and suddenly, a woman burst through the front door. She seemed slightly startled at seeing me, as I don't believe she expected someone to be in the office. She said hello cheerfully enough, and then asked, "Can I help you?"

I exclaimed, "I am here to jump." I am not sure how well my bravado came across in my voice. She gave me a brochure explaining the different jump options. I chose the 'top-of-the-line package with the video and the photos.

Once decided, she gave me a multi-page contract to review and sign. Within one glance at the first page of the contract, the excitement dwindled, and fear crept in like it belonged next to me in my seat. There was one line in the contract which seemed to jump off the page and grab my attention.

"Who would you like to have contacted in the unlikely event of your death?"

As I turned every page, my stomach turned with it. Each entry got worse on every page, but having come this far, I read and signed every page of that contract. After signing my life away, I whipped out my credit card, paid my fee, and was ready to go. Then reality set in again that I was about to pay for the thrill of a lifetime, risking my existence.

The little negative voice inside my head got louder, screaming: "What if something goes wrong?", "What if your parachute is faulty?", "What is the safety record of this company?" My heart raced at a feverish pitch, and my legs felt like lead.

Suddenly, my fear session was interrupted by a short man in a jumpsuit. He said, "Hi, I am Joe, and I will be your instructor." "Follow me!" I stood up and shook Joe's hand, then followed him out of the office and into the hangar. He pointed towards a rack of jumpsuits and instructed me to take one. After trying on several suits, I found one that fit well.

While in the hangar, other people were preparing to jump. I noticed they were in two groups, one comprising people with their gear on, who were smiling and conversing. These were people who had jumped before and were back for more.

Then there was the second group. The group of people appeared nervous and were fumbling while getting into their gear. I noticed that there was little eye contact or talk among this group. Each member was deep in thought about the events that were about to occur. The instructor appeared again. He explained how to enter the plane, the seating order, and everything else we needed to know.

I was doing a "Tandem Jump," where the instructor is strapped to the skydiver. Joe was going to be my instructor. Then, he instructed us on how to exit the plane, showing us the hand signals we needed to know while in the air. I focused on every word and committed his instructions to memory as if my life depended on it.

Before long, it was time to go to the runway and board the plane. I had a nervous smile on my face, both excited and scared all at once. I walked towards the runway. There were benches near the runway where I immediately sat down. I daydreamed about what it would be like to be over two miles up in the air with only fabric, rope, and air between me and the ground. Joe appeared, and I stood up, and he clipped his suit to mine. He looked me right in the eye and said, "Are you ready?" I said, "Yes, let's do it!"

The plane's propellers spun. After a minute, the plane taxied over to where the benches were, and we began boarding the plane. There were no seats, and the plane was about the size of a school bus. It had windows along both sides and was very cramped.

I had to enter on my knees as there was only a 4-foot clearance inside the plane and being six feet tall with Joe strapped to my back, it was very difficult to maneuver. Once inside, I was in the very last seat. The engines were running, making it very loud, so I could barely hear. After radio calls between the pilot and the hangar, we taxied out. Slowly, at first, we picked up speed. A few bumps and we were air-born!

The ride seemed to take forever. We climbed to fourteen thousand feet, which is about two miles up. There was a loud buzzer after an excruciatingly boring ride. A red light flashed, indicating that it was time! The door opened, and one by one, each of the experienced divers exited the plane.

There was a tap on my right shoulder; it was Joe, signaling that we were next. I moved towards the door. I got my first glimpse of sky, and my heart raced towards my throat. My adrenaline was pumping. I kneeled, my face out the door, looking like a puppy with its head poked out of a car window. I could hear Joe counting down behind me, "Three, two, one," and then suddenly, I saw flashes of blue, and the wind was in my face full force.

The ground looked like a painting; it didn't seem real. This was my most amazing experience. Free falling from two miles up was the ultimate ride for a roller coaster junkie like me. I felt Joe tap me on my shoulder. With all the excitement, I had forgotten that Joe was with me.

He pressed one of my arms down, and I lifted the other arm, and we spun. Then I raised one arm and flattened the other, and we spun in the opposite direction. The photographer whizzed past me while snapping my picture. I gave him a "thumbs up" sign as he sped past. I was grinning from ear to ear.

Once again, I felt a tap on my shoulder, signaling me he was about to pull the cord, which would discharge the chute. Joe pulled the cord, and with a violent jerk, I was suddenly thrust upward about 500 feet. It felt like I had been shot out of a cannon. The chute filled with air and slowed my descent.

Now, I was floating slowly to the ground below, and the view was unbelievable. I could see inland to the Atlantic. The ground was getting closer; now, I could see cars, houses, and even cows on a nearby farm. They were the size of ants. Joe pointed out different landmarks along the skyline.

Listening to him talk, my attention waned as my mind wandered. Re-living the free fall I had just experienced, a surge of power enveloped me, as if I could conquer the world. Never have I felt so alive. Silly thoughts about earlier fears surfaced, the same fears that had weighed my legs down as I boarded the plane. Those fears almost robbed me of this exhilarating experience. I pondered how many other opportunities fear had snatched away from me.

On that frosty November morning, my life changed forever. Fear is no longer a jailor, which keeps me from experiencing life.

Understanding Fear

Fear is a natural response to perceived danger, designed to protect us from harm. However, in modern society, fear often manifests as irrational worries and anxieties that keep us from reaching our full potential. By understanding the underlying causes of our fears and recognizing them as products of our mind's creations, we can dismantle their grip on our lives.

Cultivating Courage

As Loretta Lynch famously said, "Courage is not the absence of fear, but the willingness to act despite it." Cultivating courage involves stepping outside our comfort zones, taking risks, and facing our fears head-on. Courage embraces vulnerability and the unknown with an open heart and mind. By acknowledging our fears and confronting them with courage and determination, we can transcend our limitations and unlock our true potential.

Challenging Limiting Beliefs

Many fears are rooted in limiting beliefs and negative self-talk that undermine our confidence and self-worth. By challenging these beliefs and reframing our thoughts in a more empowering way, we can shift our perspective and reclaim our power. Instead of focusing on what could go wrong, we can focus on what we can learn and how we can grow from our experiences.

Embracing Failure as a Steppingstone to Success

Failure is often feared as the ultimate humiliation, but it's an essential part of the learning process. By reframing failure as a steppingstone to success and embracing it as an opportunity for growth and self-discovery, we can overcome the fear of failure and pursue our dreams with confidence and resilience. Each setback teaches valuable lessons and strengthens our resolve to persevere in adversity.

Practicing Mindfulness and Self-Compassion

Mindfulness and self-compassion are powerful tools for managing fear and anxiety. By practicing mindfulness, we can cultivate a greater awareness of our thoughts and emotions and develop the ability to respond to them with compassion and understanding. Self-compassion allows us to be kind to ourselves in moments of fear and self-doubt, reminding us we are worthy of love and acceptance, just as we are.

Fear is a natural part of the human experience, but it doesn't have to dictate the course of our lives. By understanding fear, cultivating courage, challenging limiting beliefs, embracing failure, and practicing mindfulness and self-compassion, we can overcome our fears and live authentically with courage and confidence. Remember, the only way to conquer fear is to face it head-on and rise above it with grace and resilience.

About Courtney Gale, CCHt, NLPP, PTT, CSC

Courtney Gale, Chief Empowerment Officer at New Level of Possible Coaching, is a certified life coach, speaker, and author specializing in helping individuals "Find their Why" and develop empowering belief systems and habits. As a veteran honorably discharged by both the US Marine Corps and Army National Guard, Courtney brings a disciplined and dedicated approach to coaching.

With certifications in Hypnotherapy, NLP, and Ikigai, Courtney offers a unique blend of expertise. He empowers clients to overcome obstacles and achieve fulfillment through self-discovery. His compassionate approach, coupled with proven methods, positions him as a trusted coach in personal development.

Courtney is committed to facilitating transformative change offering services such as Ikigai Coaching, Activation Method, Hypnosis, NLP, TIME Techniques, EFT, and Success Coaching. He believes everyone possesses the resources to create a fulfilling life and is passionate about helping them tap into their unlimited potential.

Get Courtney's gift: www.mind-book.net/gift/Courtney

Divine Human Beings

Master Your Mind, Stand in Your Power, Create Your Reality

By Cynthia A. Isaac, CCHt, NLPP, PTT, CSC, EFT

Then God said, "Let us make human beings in our image and likeness. And let them rule over the fish in the sea and the birds in the sky, over the tame animals, over all the earth and over all the small crawling animals on the earth." Gen. 1:26 NIV.

Then the LORD God took dust from the ground and formed a man from it. He breathed the breath of life into the man's nostrils, and the man *became a living being*. Gen. 2:7 NIV.

Then the LORD God made a woman from the rib he had taken out of the man, and he brought her to the man. The man said, "This is now bone of my bones and flesh of my flesh; she shall be called 'woman,' for she was taken out of man." That is why a man leaves his father and mother and is united with his wife, and they become one flesh. Gen. 2:22-24 NIV.

You've probably heard these scriptures since childhood and you believed them, right? So, here we have God forming mankind (soul) from a lump of dust, breathing life (spirit) into him. Not just *any* breath, but the breath of life.

Do You Know Who You Are?

You and I are human beings unlike no other creatures on the earth; made in the image and in the likeness of God. In all the

191

ways God could have designed the human body, he included lungs and the capacity to breathe in (inhale) and breathe out (exhale). The automatic rise and fall of your chest cavity are wonderful reminders of the breath of God — the life of God flowing through you.

Without the breath of God and the ability to breathe, there would be no life. It is the Spirit of God's desire to keep you filled with the breath of life. As you surrender yourself and your life to God, you receive all the benefits God has for you. As humans, you make choices and there are consequences for the choices you make.

God spoke and created human beings on earth so he could experience himself. You are an aspect of God's love experiencing life; thus, a God. Speak and create your reality.

Like Rumi, the poet says, "You are not a drop in the ocean; you are the entire ocean in a drop."

An Undeniable Truth

You are *more* than a human being. You are a Divine being, a creator, a living soul, creative consciousness, a force of life, essence, and presence. Able to transcend and transmute all the conditioning and limitations that this world has tried to put on you and make you believe. You are endowed with the *same* creative power, and the possibility of speaking your world into existence. You are created whole and complete, perfect in every way; nothing lacking, nothing missing.

It's your birthright to live and experience an abundant life on earth. Being human means creating your own reality based on your individual energetic vibration and frequency. You came into life to learn, grow, and evolve; living through your own perceptions and conscious behavior, you ascend to attain your full potential. You create reality by what you think, what you believe, what others tell you, and by what you experience in life.

So, if you look in the mirror or look at your life and don't like what you see, the only person who is responsible is you. By denying yourself your birthright and refusing to live up to your potential, you are choosing to live beneath your privileges. Either you are unaware of it, have forgotten that you've been blessed with it, or lack the ability to put it to work for you. Stop denying yourself the life, love, and power that you are.

Imagine who you could become if you believed all things are possible and nothing that you desire will be withheld from you? If you developed a healthy mindset of resiliency and self-awareness; empowered in your own God-given abilities and self-actualization, there would be nothing and no one that could stop you from being, doing, and having your heart's desire, providing your desires line up with the principles and nature of the All. These truths penetrate your being on all levels: physically, mentally, emotionally, energetically, and spiritually, regardless of who you are.

Although this writing uses God, know that whoever and whatever your ideal of God is; Creator, Divine, Spirit, Source, Universe, The All, the Great I AM, Gaia; it qualifies. This is not about religion, race, creed, nationalities, cultures, or gender. It's about human beings. If you allow yourself to master your mind, listen with a pure heart, and open wide to receiving, you will become embodied with inner truth and consciousness that defies everything you have been led to believe in yourself and your life.

Be Still and Know

Consider taking the time to slow down, go within. Take a deep dive into this knowing; understand it reveals layers of your existence that you may never have noticed unfolding. Allow yourself to expand beyond the physical, beyond the mental, into the energetic and spiritual realms: into the initial existence; beginning life as you know it.

In society, most people focus on material, external things and put emphasis on accomplishments represented by labels. They give importance to certain words that do not compare to the true aspect of who you are within. At the level of your soul is where truth lives and where life dictates your true identity, which transcends all superficiality. Your identity in the world is according to your title, position, name, age, occupation, the house, or neighborhood you live in, or the car you drive. None of which describes your value, worth, essence, or your life experiences. It's these very labels, and those adopted or placed upon you, that keep you stuck in limited situations with no expectation of rising above what you have been conditioned to believe. To find real freedom, you must free your mind from these limitations, open your consciousness to new possibilities, and create new realities.

The thief comes to steal, kill, and destroy the connection you have with the Divine. He's been coming for eons, and he will continue coming as long as humans conditioned by worldly systems will live beneath divinity and forgo your innate human rights given by God: freedom, equality, and dignity. These are given to all humans, made in the image of God. These rights are not earned, but divinely ordained.

The world has been controlled under a patriarchy system of relationships, beliefs, and values that are embedded in the political, social, and economic systems that structure gender inequality between men and women. Currently, things may be on shaky foundations and feel disorienting. In actuality, the world is transitioning between the old patriarchy ways of capitalism, extraction culture, and white supremacy and creating new systems where more equality and mutual thriving becomes possible. This awkward space lends itself to questioning, constraints and potentially negative inherited behaviors.

About two million years ago, human society was matriarchal, and women were respected and worshipped as goddesses. Women were the givers of life and were sacred beings, and older women were regarded as the strongest pillars in the society. Many matriarchal societies where women rule still exist in China, Indonesia, Costa Rica, Kenya, the Indigenous culture in Hawaii, and many Native American tribes.

However, 3000 to 3500 years ago, there was a move from matriarchy to patriarchy societies where males were given advantages. Women were excluded from equal positions of power, paid less for work of equal value, and more likely experienced poverty and unequal access to resources, goods, and services. Intentionally moving further away from the true feminine *Shekinah* aspect of God.

Patriarchy as a power structure predates capitalism and exists under a variety of other modes, such as slavery, feudalism, and capitalism. In this system, the work is done by a majority, yet all the wealth produced is controlled by only 1%. This is exploitation and causes ill will as people figure out they're locked into a system. It's time to change the system by acknowledging the impact of patriarchy on society and on relationships, by understanding where patriarchy comes from and by taking responsibility for gender inequality and using a more feminist approach.

In the meantime, how do you navigate this space and keep resources, co-creating and shining just the same? Perhaps it's time to re-evaluate these systems and the narratives that uphold them, starting with the women.

Rise of the Divine Feminine

You live in a world of illusion in a matrix where there is a set of rules that determine how things work. Understanding these rules is key to success and you can learn to hack the codes by mastering your mind. However, accepting the status quo versus breaking free requires "knowing thyself," trusting and believing in who you are, and in the power you possess within. Your decisions hold significance because you are unique, and your individuality is valid.

You are the New Earth; the new future is already happening. There is no fine line between the past and the better future, instead there's a gradual expanding, a powerful awakening, a gentle empowerment taking place in the hearts, minds, and souls of the people who are choosing to reclaim ancient wisdom and restore harmony for the earth. The overwhelm, grief, anxiety, and despair over climate are all logical responses. Hope, holy rage, a sense of urgency, and the possibility of coming together in the community can complement these feelings.

Anticipate an unraveling of old thought forms, ancestral core beliefs, outdated perspectives, and unhealthy behaviors. Processing this is substantial as the old constructs crack and break apart, unveiling the budding true you. Releasing the old, outdated ego persona is necessary. It's been an artificial construct since childhood, serving the illusion. Layers of coping mechanisms and reactionary responses have been its composition, crafted for safety in a reality of separation. Its dominance over thoughts, emotions, choices, or actions in daily life can no longer persist.

Empowered to Make a Difference

February was Black History month; in remembrance of Dr. MLK and Malcom X, the forerunners, and other eminent men and women who risked their lives to create a better future for African Americans. It's over fifty years later; can you emphatically say their death was not in vain?

March is Women's History month, recalling Sojourner Truth's speech, 'Ain't I a Woman,' in which she asked: "Where did your Christ come from? From God, and a woman. Man had nothing to do with it. If women want to turn this world back right side up, then the men ought to let them." As a Divine Feminine, you are called to love yourself completely and join with your Divine Masculine counterpart.

You lead your families and communities to a new future where no one is denied their birthrights, excluded, or left behind. It's up to you, Divine Human Beings as a collective, to take authority and stand in your power, refusing to accept less than you deserve. You do whatever it takes to live together in harmony and peace.

When one segment struggles, you all struggle. There's a difference between experiencing trauma and living a traumatized life.

Refuse to be defeated.

Recommit to your true self: beings of joy, love, beauty, peace, self-confidence, self-awareness. Only you can change your life and your children's lives by refusing to live a status quo and doing whatever it takes to master your mind and be empowered in your ability to live the abundant life; your birthright.

As your mentor and guide, my purpose is to love you, to serve you, and to encourage you to love yourself fully. It's my desire to support you on this journey of empowerment, releasing limiting beliefs, conditionings, societal norms, and fear. Remember, fighting for your limitations only means you get to keep them. And how's that working for you?

If you're ready to let go of everything you think you know about yourself, open to release what no longer serves you, ready to love yourself totally, ready to enjoy all the God-given birthrights you deserve, then I invite you to join the collective in leading humanity with love. Grab your gifts and let's connect soon.

About Cynthia A Isaac, CCHt, NLPP, PTT, CSC, EFT

Cynthia A Isaac is a skilled Mentor, NLP Practitioner, Hypnotherapist, and Transformation Coach, with over 10 years of experience in the field. Graduating from Transform Destiny with certifications in NLP, Hypnotherapy, & Emotion Codes, Cynthia has dedicated her career to helping Women of Color: professionals, business owners, and entrepreneurs, shift mindsets, transform their lives, and create new self-empowered opportunities for growth and success.

As founder of Divine Human Beings, Cynthia uses her expertise to guide her clients through powerful processes that facilitate transformation. Her compassionate approach allows women to break through societal norms, overcome limiting beliefs, and unlock their full potential.

Besides her work as a practitioner, Cynthia is a best-selling author, sharing her wisdom and insights on the TRUTH of who you are, knowing your birthright, and living an abundant life. Her commitment to empower women to live their best authentic lives shines through in all aspects of her work, inspiring those she serves to embrace self-love, pursue their goals, and leave a legacy.

Cynthia is a trusted guide and mentor for those seeking the confidence to build healthy families and communities.

Get Cynthia's free gift: www.mind-book.net/gift/Cynthia

The Sea of Hope
Overcoming Adversities Through the Power of the Mind
By Félicia "Faith" Hart

Have you ever been told you are not enough? Have you ever thought about how life would be, if only? Do you ever feel powerless or trapped? Are you hoping for laughter and smiles again, but shame and anxiety is holding you back from a better tomorrow? Are you tired of crying yourself to sleep, unsure of the feelings you have? That little child inside is lost, wondering how to be set free. Is there safety? That child sees nowhere to turn and is too afraid to speak up. Am I enough? Why me?

Cutting across this fear is the light shining on the path where you can lean on the higher power to guide you to find help, to know that yes, deep down, something is wrong, and clarity is needed.

Fear, He is a liar:

You are enough!

You are beautiful!

You are smart!

You are stronger than you think!

You are worthy and more than enough! What has stopped you in the past does not have to stop you today!

Listen to your inner voice when told you are inadequate and cannot believe you have it within you. What is said is a lie because you are more than you know; we are all called for greatness with a higher purpose.

It is natural to feel uncomfortable when stepping out of your normalcy of life. However, remember that courage is not the absence of fear; it is the decision that something else is more important.

Affirmation: "I am courageous and willing to face my fears."

Are you dealing with fear, shame, anxiety, or limited beliefs holding you back from achieving your goals and affecting your health?

This was once me. Lost and now found—blinded and now can see.

> *In the heart of a picturesque town, amidst the gentle embrace of the creeks, mountains, tall green trees, turkeys, cows, deer, and wildcats crossing roads, lived a young, fruitful lady with a driven spirit. A ballet dancer, with each pirouette and plié, sought to escape the confines of her tumultuous world—a world shrouded in abuse behind closed doors. Behind the façade of elegance and beauty, lays a hidden world of pain and despair. In a web of abusive narcissistic torment, her spirit weighed down by fear, shame, and a crippling sense of hopelessness. She longed for peace, safety,*

and belonging, but the darkness of her reality seemed impenetrable.

The scars of abuse ran deep, weaving a tangled web of self-doubt and insecurity around her fragile spirit. She dared not hope for a better tomorrow, for the mere thought filled her with a paralyzing dread. Toxic, cruel words by her mate cut more deeply than any blade. She danced on fragile glass, tiptoeing around temperamental whims while yearning for a sanctuary where she could find solace and belonging. Instead, spending nights on her knees in tears of desperation, praying for an out.

Day after day, she danced through the motions of her life, her heart heavy with the burden of her secret torment. She dared not speak of the abuse that ravaged her soul, for the fear of judgment and reprisal loomed like a dark shadow over her. The consumption with navigating the treacherous waters of her tumultuous marriage, her every step dictated by the fear of setting off her husband's explosive temper. The sound of her children's screams echoed through the halls, and voices drowned out by the suffocating silence of fear.

In a small town where everyone knew everyone else's business, she felt trapped in a suffocating cage of societal expectations. She wore a mask of perfection, smiling brightly for the world to see, protecting her children while her heart cried out for salvation. But deep within the recesses of her soul, a glimmer of hope flickered like a distant beacon in the night. She longed for a natural sanctuary where she could find the strength to break free from the chains of abuse, but the path to freedom seemed shrouded in darkness.

One fateful evening, as the sun dipped below the horizon, she was drawn to the seashore, where the crashing waves whispered tales of untold strength and resilience. With each step she took, the salty breeze kissed her cheeks, offering a gentle reminder of the beauty that still existed in the world.

As she stood on the sandy shore, her gaze fixated on the endless expanse of the ocean; she felt a flicker of courage stir within her soul. The rhythmic symphony of the waves washed away her fears, leaving a sense of calm and clarity she had not felt in years. In that moment of stillness, she closed her eyes and allowed herself to dream of a life free from the shackles of abuse—a life that danced to the beat of her own heart, unburdened by the weight of her past. She imagined herself surrounded by laughter and joy, the echoes of children playing in the distance like music to her ears.

With each breath she took, she felt the tendrils of fear and shame loosen their grip, replaced by a newfound sense of hope and determination. She knew the road ahead would not be easy, but she also knew she was not alone. The sea whispered words of encouragement, reminding her she had the strength and resilience to weather any storm. As she walked away from the shore, her heart filled with resolve; she knew she was no longer a victim but a warrior fighting for her liberation. Cultivating a mindset of resilience and empowerment allowed her to face the darkness with unwavering courage.

Though the road ahead was long and uncertain, she walked it with her head held high, knowing that she was not defined by her past but by the strength and courage that burned within her soul. As she looked towards the horizon, she knew that one day, she would emerge from the shadows, bathed in the light of a new dawn—a beacon of hope and inspiration for others who dared to dream of a brighter future.

As she embraced her newfound freedom, she vowed to use her experience to help others living in the shadows of abuse. She became an advocate for survivors, speaking out against domestic violence and offering support to those in need, bringing inner light to one person at a time, making a difference. And though the scars of her past would always remain, she found solace in knowing that she had overcome the darkest of nights to bask in the dawn of a new day.

To have a broken wing and want to fly but trapped or lost - To look back and say I am now flying free again like a butterfly, my symbol of strength is my testimony. My story, one of a professional dancer from age 14 who took on the world and lived out her dream into her late twenties, landed herself in a twisted and fearful marriage that destroyed her on so many unfathomable levels.

However, there is a new beginning: "There is no fear in Love. But perfect Love drives out fear because fear has to do with punishment. The one who fears is not made perfect in Love." - *John 4:18 Holy Bible (NIV)*

A new life is possible with the shift of empowerment and mastery of the mind!

The journey towards readiness for change begins with acknowledging "I can't," transitioning gradually to "I'm considering it," signifying a shift in mindset. Progressing further, one adopts the determination of "I will," followed by the essential step of planning for potential obstacles.

As one proceeds, the importance of having support and accountability becomes apparent, fortifying inner strength. With a firm commitment expressed as "Yes, I'm doing it," coupled with diligent self-monitoring and maintenance, the path to change becomes clearer. Even as challenges arise, persisting with "I'm still doing it" demonstrates resilience and growing attachment to the process.

Ultimately, reaching the point of declaring, "I like this, and I want to keep doing it" reflects an embrace of newfound habits and a desire for continuity. Each step in this journey contributes to the transformative process, culminating in the empowering realization of "stepping into a higher version of oneself."

When is it your day to step out in faith and believe in yourself?

A wise mentor once said, "I don't wait for change; I am the change."

Sometimes, we must look back and heal to go forward.

Reflect, Release, and Rise Above.

When you have lost your voice and are afraid to speak, placing your voice on the pages of a journal soothes your soul until your inner warrior comes out and is ready to stand strong. As you turn the page, close the book each day for a new beginning, until you are ready to let go.

There is REAL hope, and you are not alone. You have advocates, attorneys, friends (if not family), and yes, protection. Your voice matters and deserves to be heard!

There are local and national resources.

"Everyone deserves healthy relationships!" National Domestic Violence Hotline 1-800-799-SAFE (7233)

A theologian named Reinhold Niebuhr is believed to have written the Serenity Prayer: "God, Grant me the serenity to accept the things I cannot change, the courage to change the things I can, and the wisdom to know the difference."

It is time to get up with confidence and seek your inspiration to reach inner peace and outer abundance. You deserve freedom, so hold on to hope, believe, and rise up with faith.

"Nothing is impossible; the word itself says that I AM POSSIBLE!"–Audrey Hepburn

Start with the love of thyself. You are beautiful, mighty, and strong, even when you feel weak. Your inner warrior is inside you, like when you were a child who believed in anything and everything possible for you to dream and chase for a smile. Hold on to the smallest gifts of life, like the simplicity of stopping to smell a rose, or hear the rain splat. A small step of faith can go a long way in the dark. Like a dancer who has fallen on stage and instead acts like it was part of the dance flawlessly. She stands strong and keeps dancing with grace!

As I sit upon this crescent rock and ponder, Sprinkles of mist come upon me, White as snow yet crisp in beauty. Each high surf is created uniquely. It is an iridescent sight, like a raging storm waiting to happen as waves crash along the shore.

Our life is like the ocean. It is up to you to decide how to ride the wave. To be dragged into a storm or waves of turmoil, you may feel alone, but keep your head high, because a brighter tomorrow awaits. Remember, you are loved! So ask yourself honestly: When is it time to fly again, to let your wings wholeheartedly fly free to be you again?

Isaiah 40:31- Holy Bible (NIV) says, "Those who hope in the Lord will renew their strength. They will soar on wings like eagles. They will run and not grow weary. They will walk and not faint."

It is time the cage opened; let your wings spread and say goodbye to fear. My program, "Align with Faith" is built on the foundation of God's Kingdom, knowing that real Love is out there. Let not thy mind deny the thought of Your higher power; God is but Love. The peace of God is shining in you now.

Admit the Truth. The truth is so hard to speak when your voice is constantly shut down. Accepting the truth can be heartbreaking because you must face reality and the fear of judgment. I am not asking you to judge yourself; clear the decks and start building on what is honest and not a gray area. Name "the shame" and have courage to speak up. Start writing and close the books of yesterday!

Time is of the essence; it is time to recognize, reflect, and rise from pain to power, letting go to greatness. My new purposes are embodiment, resilience, prosperity, pursuing happiness with wisdom and grace, and bringing His Light into each client's life. If you are reading this, I hope your story will and can have peace. I believe in you, and I am here to help overcome any adversities in life side-by-side as your coach.

Say Yes to a new you! Gifts await at AlignwithFaith.com.

With Love & Light, Your Coach Faith

About Félicia "FAITH" Hart

 Félicia "FAITH" Hart, founder of Align with Faith, is passionate about empowering women through self-care, well-being, and guiding them to access their inner strength and adapt to a brighter future.

Faith received training from the Health Coach Institute, Institute of Integrative Nutrition, and Yoga Works and is nationally board-certified.

Her certifications include Mastery Health Coach, Emotional Eating, Gut Health, and Mastery Life Success Coach, and she has been featured on ABC, CBS, FOX, and NBC. Drawing from her background as a Professional Dancer, Pilates Teacher, and Essential Oil Specialist, Faith offers a unique blend of knowledge and experience in her coaching practice.

Faith remains dedicated to ongoing learning, staying informed on the latest trends, and research in health and wellness. Her holistic coaching approach addresses the root causes of issues by aligning physical, emotional, and spiritual well-being, equipping clients with tools for vibrant health and a fulfilling life. When not coaching, Faith cherishes time with her four children, grateful for their unwavering support.

Use coupon code "SEAOFHOPE8" at the link below to get your gift for free.

Get Faith's free gift: www.mind-book.net/gift/Faith

How to Achieve Anything You Put Your Mind To

By Michael Stevenson,
Master Coach and Master Trainer of NLP

We know quite a bit about success in Neuro-Linguistic Programming because it's all we study. NLP is a field of modeling excellence and then teaching those models to others so they can be successful, too.

As someone who has walked the rocky path from struggle to success, I've experienced firsthand how mastering our minds can unlock doors to achievement and fulfillment we never thought possible.

We will explore **The Principles of Success from Neuro-Linguistic Programming**, a framework that has not only transformed my life but has also been the cornerstone of countless others' journeys toward personal and professional greatness. These principles are simple yet profound, easy to understand, but require commitment to apply.

What I'm about to share with you is the roadmap to achieving anything you want in life. Follow this roadmap exactly and relentlessly, and you will succeed at anything you set your mind to.

Step 1: Know Your Outcome

Your subconscious mind is a powerful force in achievement. But to tap into the vast resources available at an unconscious level, you must know what you want, not what you don't want.

Now, when I use the word "know" in this context, it doesn't mean to just intellectually be able to describe it in words. Instead, it means you want an "internal representation" of the outcome as if it's happening right now.

An internal representation is the unique and personal way you experience and represents your goals and desires through your internal senses. It's how you create a mental blueprint of what you want to achieve, not just in one modality but encompassing all the ways you perceive the world: what you see, hear, feel, and even taste or smell.

Engaging all your senses is crucial to harness the power of knowing your outcome.

Imagine you're crafting a multi-sensory experience of your desired future, where you are the director, the screenwriter, and the star. For some, this movie might be more vivid in visual scenes; for others, it could be the dialog and sounds that bring it to life, or the sensations and emotions they feel throughout the story. Whatever way you experience it, is right for you.

This movie is not just any story—it's your story, detailed and rich, unfolding exactly as you wish.

Let's Break it Down:

1. See: What does the picture of your success look like? Imagine the environment, the people around you, the details of the setting where your goals have been realized. This isn't just about seeing yourself in this scenario, but noticing the colors, the light, and the elements that make the scene real.

2. Hear: What sounds accompany your achievement? These could be the words of congratulations from people you respect, the sound of your own voice brimming with confidence, or even the ambient sounds in the background of your success. These sounds make the experience more vivid and anchor your success.

3. Feel: What sensations and emotions flood through you as you reach your goals? It might be a sense of warmth, a rush of exhilaration, or a deep, fulfilling peace. Feeling the outcome as if it's happening now bridges the gap between where you are and where you want to be.

And remember, it's important for you to know the end result — the moment it happens.

Knowing your outcome in such a vivid and encompassing way does something remarkable—it sets the stage for your subconscious mind to align with your conscious goals. It's like planting a flag in the terrain of your future achievements. Your mind recognizes this flag, this detailed sensory experience, as a destination. And just like a skilled navigator uses stars to guide a ship, your mind uses this internal representation to steer you toward your goals.

Once you know your outcome, the next step is to dissociate from that internal representation. This means stepping out of your body and experiencing it from a second-person perspective in your mind. This is a crucial step to letting your subconscious mind know that you are not fantasizing but giving it an end goal to achieve.

Step 2: Take Real Action

To achieve anything in life, we must act. That's common sense. But it's pivotal to recognize that action — the kind that propels us toward our dreams — occurs not just on one plane but intersects across four crucial dimensions: spiritual, emotional, mental, and physical.

Spiritual: This plane is where your purpose and deepest values live. It's the "why" behind your goals. It's about connecting with something greater than yourself, whether that's a higher power, a set of spiritual beliefs, or a deep-seated sense of purpose. This alignment ensures that your actions are not just effective, but meaningful.

Emotional: Emotions fuel our motivation and drive. On this plane, acting means managing and harnessing your emotions to support your journey. It involves cultivating resilience, passion, and a positive mindset, as well as releasing negativity like limiting beliefs and values conflicts.

Mental: Mental action is about preparing, strategizing, and mentally rehearsing your steps towards your goal. It's where you break down your outcome into actionable steps and mentally equip yourself to face challenges. This plane is crucial for transforming the abstract into the actionable, setting the stage for physical execution.

Physical: Physical action is where the rubber meets the road; it's the tangible steps you take in the real world toward your goal. This is where ideas, plans, and intentions are transformed into concrete achievements. Real action on the physical plane is the most visible and measurable form of progress. It's writing the book, building the business, the daily practice of skills, and the consistent effort towards health and well-being.

Understanding that real action <u>only</u> takes place on the physical plane but is supported and enriched by the spiritual, emotional, and mental planes offers a holistic approach to achieving your goals. To take real action means engaging with all four planes, ensuring they are in alignment with the physical actions you take, being informed, and fueled by the spiritual, emotional, and mental groundwork you've laid.

Step 3: Pay Attention to Your Results

This concept is not just about observing outcomes; it's about fine tuning into the feedback of every action, using all your senses. It's the art of being fully present and attentive to what's happening around you and within you, recognizing both the triumphs and the setbacks as invaluable data points on your journey to success.

Sensory acuity involves using your senses to detect the subtle nuances in your progress. It's about noticing the changes in your environment, the reactions from others, and the internal shifts in your own thoughts and emotions.

This heightened awareness enables you to discern the obvious outcomes and the subtle cues that signal if you're moving toward your outcome.

Paying attention to your results through the lens of sensory acuity is a dynamic process. It's an ongoing dialog with your experiences, a feedback loop that informs every step you take. By embracing both the good and the bad with openness and curiosity, you unlock the ability to navigate your path with greater precision and adaptability.

Step 4: Be Willing to Change Your Behavior

If your results aren't moving you toward your outcome, or not moving you quickly enough, the next step is to be willing to change your behavior. A popular adage says "The definition of insanity is doing the same thing over and over and expecting different results."

The challenge is that sometimes behavior is hard to change on its own. For example, a person who wants to lose weight and buys a gym membership but then never goes to the gym.

We need to go deeper into the subconscious mind as the greatest changes happen deep within, and then behavior changes on its own. Here are the levels of change you can make from the most transformation to the least:

Identity: Change to become who you want to be. For example, you must become an author to write a book. You cannot wait to have a book to call yourself an author. Similarly, you must become wealthy to attract wealth. Even if you're poor, adopt the identity of wealth first.

Values: Elevate the importance of those things that will facilitate your achievement. For example, to get in shape, health and fitness must become important to you. Unfortunately, for most people, convenience is their primary driver. But this must change if you want success.

Beliefs: Often it is limiting beliefs or conflicting beliefs that hold us back. While beliefs are powerful, they are just thoughts you think with conviction. They are simply thoughts you trust to be true. They can be changed. Tools such as Neuro-Linguistic Programming and hypnotherapy are fantastic at eliminating negative beliefs.

Potential: Sometimes, you must learn something new to change your behavior. This includes things such as experimenting, taking courses, watching videos, and reading books to enrich your behaviors.

What if you don't know what to change? Change *anything*.

Be willing to experiment and try different things. The person with the most flexibility and willingness to do what it takes to succeed will always win.

Step 5: Focus on Excellence

One of the most destructive limiting beliefs that pervades our society is the belief that we must be "perfect."

Perfection is not only fiction but also a trap. It's an imaginary, inflexible, unattainable ideal that we are supposed to compare ourselves to. It often creates "analysis paralysis" and makes most people freeze, take no action at all.

Instead, focus on *excellence*.

Excellence is not a comparison to an external ideal, but a comparison of who you are now to who you were before. It's a healthy competition with yourself.

Look at anyone who has achieved greatness and you will find they are always seeking to outdo themselves in a relentless pursuit of growth, not perfection.

When you focus on excellence, you commit yourself to a practice of constant and never-ending improvement, always being willing to experiment and realizing that there is no such thing as "failure." There is only "feedback."

Step 6: Live With Gratitude and Integrity

The last component of achievement has to do with your attitude toward achievement.

Often, people want to change in life because they are "sick and tired" of where they are. But focusing on what you don't want will just create more of what you don't want.

Gratitude is like "rocket fuel" to achievement (and to the Law of Attraction if you're a follower).

Gratitude doesn't mean being grateful for the lack. It means finding the abundance where you're not seeing it and focusing on that. Whatever you focus on expands.

Integrity is paramount to long-term achievement because all success depends on relationships. My definition is three-fold: say what you mean, do what you say, and always seek win-win outcomes.

Putting It into Action

The beauty of The Principles of Success is that they're not just a roadmap — they're also a diagnostic tool. If there's something in your life that isn't working, come back and look at the principles and you'll find one of these steps is lacking.

When you focus on and follow these steps with full commitment, you'll achieve more than ever before.

About Michael Stevenson, Master Trainer of NLP

Michael Stevenson is the Founder and CEO of Transform Destiny and a Master Trainer of Neuro-Linguistic Programming (NLP). With over 25 years of experience, he has helped countless coaches, therapists, and business owners take their lives and businesses to the next level.

Michael is a best-selling author of multiple books and co-starred in the documentary The Evolution of Success. He has a passion for helping people become the best versions of themselves and to live their dreams. He often uses NLP techniques to help his clients reach their goals.

Michael is an expert at helping people understand how to use their minds and language to create positive change in their lives. His unique approach to personal and professional development has earned him the respect of his peers and clients alike. He is a highly sought-after speaker at conferences and workshops around the world.

Michael is committed to helping people achieve success and reach their dreams. His passion is helping them learn how to use their minds to create the life they desire. He believes anyone can reach their goals with the right tools and attitude. He is committed to helping others reach their dreams and live the life they've always wanted.

Get Michael's free gift: www.mind-book.net/gift/Michael